# ALL TEENS: DESTINED FOR GREATNESS!

*Pam Mullarkey, Ph.D.*

Xulon PRESS

# ACKNOWLEDGMENTS

First and foremost, I thank God Almighty, because without Him, Project SOS would not have existed and none of these true stories would have been told.

Secondly, I want to thank my wonderful, devoted husband, David Mullarkey, who has been my support system since the day we said, "I do" in 1969. David and our family of two sons have sacrificed a lot for me to follow the calling God gave me in 1993.

Thirdly, I want to thank all of the dedicated, hard working staff and volunteers who have been the instruments that God has used to change our youth culture for the better. Together, we have helped hundreds of thousands of teenagers and their families live healthy lives with few regrets.

Fourthly, I want to thank Kathy Osgood, my friend, the poet who always hears from God and translates His words into simplistic messages that all people can understand and love.

Lastly, I thank all of the individuals, board members, families, churches, foundations, state government, and the federal government for believing in our vision enough to financially support it. I'm glad we didn't let you down.

Together we are winning the battle and will continue to win as long as there are generous donors that believe in our youth culture.

In conclusion, this book would never have been written without the generosity of board member Charlie Christie and his wife, Rebecca. They flew me to their mountain home outside Denver so I could focus totally on this book. My desire is that this book would ignite a fire in the hearts of our youth to rise up and be the Daniels of their generation who choose God's ways over Hollywood's ways. I believe with all my heart that those teens who catch the fire in their hearts will lead their generation into the greatest revival our nation has ever seen.

# CONTENTS

# INTRODUCTION

By Pam Mullarkey, Ph.D.

I have had the awesome privilege of being the Founder and Executive Director of Project SOS, Inc. (Strengthening Our Students). This organization is one of the largest abstinence organizations in the nation. I have an absolutely outstanding staff of forty individuals: twenty work part-time while attending college or working; the other twenty are full-time employees. We come in all shapes, colors, sizes, and backgrounds, but we all have one thing in common: We have dedicated our lives to **change our youth culture for the better by bringing truth to our youth.** Two-thirds of our staff is under the age of twenty-five and for many, this job is their first full-time employment.

The most unique thing about these young adult staff members is that regardless of their past, they are all committed to abstinence from sex, drugs, alcohol abuse, suicide, violence, and eating disorders. How can this be when many of my staff, both past and present, have come from very sexually active lifestyles, some from drug addictions, others have tried to kill themselves, and still others have battled eating disorders? You are about to find out as you read some of their stories. These are just a few of the stories of many young adults that have worked for Project SOS since 1993.

The stories within this book are true, but the names have been changed to protect the identities of their families. Most of my staff members go on to marry, and all walk down the aisle as either a virgin or "recycled" virgins (people who returned to abstinence until marriage). All staff have made a commitment to avoid unhealthy choices and to share the tremendous advantages of living a lifestyle of freedom from regret, worry, relationship pain, abuse, addiction, and

broken hearts. They have experienced the advantages of setting a standard of excellence and helping others reach for the same high goal, not allowing others to pressure them to lower those standards.

My hope and prayer is that by reading about the lives of several of my staff, you will realize that ALL TEENS **ARE** DESTINED FOR GREATNESS. I also hope you will reach out to other teenagers, accept and love them unconditionally, and encourage them to believe their future is one of great destiny.

Every person is a unique, valuable individual filled with gifts and talents that are waiting to be discovered. Many want to do great things but have no idea where to begin. Greatness begins with an encourager, someone who overlooks the outer shell and tries to see the heart and the needs of the other person. Think about someone in your life who is an encourager. Is it a parent, teacher, coach, babysitter, friend, or family member? I pray this book will serve to encourage and empower you so that you will then share this book with a friend.

Dream big! Ask God what He wants you to do. You might be surprised by the answer. You might even be afraid of some of the dreams He is putting in your heart right now. I was scared to death when God woke me up in the middle of the night for five nights in a row and had me go to the kitchen table and write the entire plan for Project SOS. I knew the task was too big. It didn't fit into my plans, and I was not capable of starting and leading a non-profit organization, but God knew better. He believed in me and surrounded me with people to encourage and help me. Through Him and the people He has brought to Project SOS, I have been able to daily live the destiny God has planned for my life, and so can you.

The first Bible verse I ever memorized in 1993, when God's plan was laid out before me for my life, was this one: **"Fear not, for I am with you. I will uphold you with my righteous right hand."** The second verse I memorized was, **"I can do ALL things through Christ that strengthens me."**

If we could get just a small glimpse of how God sees us, then surely our insecurities and self-centeredness would truly dissolve. As God's Word tells us, **"We see through a glass dimly."** I believe we have very little knowledge and vision of the person we have been born to be, the lives we will help change, and the people our own lives will impact. THINK BIG THOUGHTS! Remember: **"All things are possible for those who love the Lord."**

No matter what you are facing in your life, no matter what may have happened to you in your past, and regardless of what you have been told, you and you alone can control your thoughts. Think BIG thoughts of taking your place to fulfill your destiny in your home, school, neighborhood, state, nation, or universe! Make this place a better place to live because of your life and your efforts. I hope with all my heart that you will catch the vision and join Project SOS in changing your youth culture for the better. Reach down from the wall of life and help pull someone else up by believing in him and encouraging him to fulfill the destiny God has planned for his life.

We are not here to merely exist. We are not here to serve ourselves only. We are here for His purposes and plans for our lives. We are here because He has planned for us to be great. If you doubt what I am saying, look down at your fingers and stop to think:

*Why am I the only person on the face of the earth with these fingerprints? Why doesn't someone else, somewhere in the world, have the same DNA, or body scent, or personality that I have?*

The answer is that you were created one of a kind. No one can replace you, because no one is exactly like you. Your life has tremendous value, and we need you and your gifts and talents. No one else can fulfill the destiny God has for your life in this world during your generation. God's Word says, **"For I know the plans I have for you. Plans to prosper you and to give you hope."** Enjoy this book and share with a friend.

# GOD'S VISION FOR PROJECT SOS

In 1993, as I was walking in my neighborhood, I was thinking about finishing my second four-year term serving on our local St. Johns County School Board located in Northeast Florida. Friends were encouraging me to run for a state house seat, others were hoping I would run for mayor if the vote passed to incorporate Ponte Vedra Beach. I loved being an elected official, because I enjoyed helping people and making changes that affected entire groups, not just individuals.

As I was contemplating my future, a neighborhood child walked up. She quickly picked up my stride, not wanting to cause me to slow down, and said, "Miss Pam, could you help me?" I kept walking and said, "Of course I will help you; what is it you need?" She said, "My best friend is pregnant and she's going to have an abortion in three days and she is really, really scared. Do you think you could tell her mother?" I immediately stopped my walking and turned to this beautiful ninth grade girl and said to her, "Of course I'll tell her mother. What's your friend's name?" She quickly gave me her name, which threw me into total shock, because I knew her mother and family very well. I quipped back to her, "Are you sure you have the right name?" Their daughter can't be pregnant!" She assured me that she knew her best friend's name and wanted to help her through her decision, fears, and worries. After thinking for a few seconds, my mind racing all the while, I promised her I would go home and contact the mother to let her know about her daughter and the decision she was about to make. I also wanted to give the family some other options if they were willing to consider them. As I stood there with that ninth-grade neighborhood girl, I had a flashback to the time I was a health teacher and had to tell several mothers the bad news about their daughters being pregnant.

Let me tell you a little bit about this neighborhood family so you can understand the shock I felt when I was told their name. Both parents had master's degrees from leading universities. They had two children, a daughter, fourteen, and a son, nine. Both children were straight "A" students. Their family had moved into this school district because of the quality of life and education they felt that St. Johns County offered. The family attended church together and never missed a soccer game, school performance, or awards ceremony for either child. They both worked within five minutes of their home so they could be there when they were needed. The parents were neighbors of ours. My husband, David, and I admired how they were raising their children, especially the grades their children were bringing home.

I cut my walk short. I didn't feel like walking much anymore. I had to do something very difficult and had to do it right then in order to have any kind of peace in my mind. I had learned by that time in my life that the longer I put something off that I didn't want to do, the bigger and more dreaded the task became. Then my mind would blow it totally out of proportion and my day would be absolutely ruined until I tackled the job. Once I had made up my mind to do the task, then a peace would re-enter my mind. Knowing that, I went to the phone and said a prayer that God would give me the words to speak in love and help the mother find strength in Him. I dialed her number and she answered, "Oh, hi, Pam. What's up?" I responded, "Can you come over to my house? I have something I need to talk to you about. Are you busy right now?" I could sense the caution in her voice as she replied, "I'll be right there." Within two minutes, she drove into my driveway. As I watched her walk to my front door, I again asked God to give me the words He wanted her to hear from my mouth.

We went back to the television room, and after we did some of the usual icebreaker chitchat, I told her, "I have something terrible to tell you. Your daughter is pregnant and is going to have an abortion in three days. She's very frightened and I wanted you to know. I think this needs to be a family decision, and I have some options if you are willing to look at them." Immediately this mother started laughing out loud. She looked right into my eyes and told me without any doubt, "Pam, my daughter can't be pregnant, she has never had a date! We don't let her date; she just turned fourteen!" I pulled up all the courage that I could find and responded, "Your daughter's best friend told me because your daughter is very frightened, and she thought you needed to know."

For the next several hours, we talked, we cried, and we looked at some of her daughter's options together. Around 9:00 that evening my friend left to go confront her daughter. As she walked out the door, I began to pray for her and her family. I knew the worse part was about to begin, but after, the future for that entire family would be better. I understood families needed to come together during times of crisis and work through their issues. I had seen too many teenagers keep secrets from their parents, causing the family dynamics to totally change. I knew from past experiences as a teacher that keeping secrets breaks down communication and increases feelings of regret and shame in the minds of teens, sometimes leading to destructive behaviors such as drugs, alcohol, suicide, abuse, or even worse.

The next morning I received a phone call from my friend. She said, "Pam, our daughter *is* pregnant and I would like to tell you what happened." I responded that I really wanted to know because I was in total shock that their beautiful, brilliant daughter could be pregnant. She continued, "When our daughter arrived as a freshman at the local high school, a senior on the football team came up to her and introduced himself. She was flattered that a senior athlete would take an interest in a ninth grader. One day, he asked her for her address and phone number and permission to come over and visit her after school sometime. She had never been asked that before so she told him, 'I guess it would be okay. I watch my little brother after school until my parents get home, sometime after 5:00.' He smiled and raced off to football practice. Within several days, he came to visit our daughter. He realized she was very shy and had no idea how to say "no" to a guy. He started sweet-talking her and, eventually, talked her into going into her bedroom and giving him her virginity. After having sex, he talked to her a little longer and then left our home before we got there. The next day at football practice he gave out copies of our daughter's name, address, and phone number. He then made the announcement to the entire team that anyone could go visit her after school before her parents got home. He told them they could have sex with her too because she didn't know how to say 'no'. He said all they needed to do was sweet talk her and she would respond the same way she had done the day before with him." The mother then concluded our conversation by adding, "She has had more than one visitor and doesn't know who the baby's father is!"

I could feel the pain in the mother's voice, but I couldn't even imagine the anger her husband must have felt toward those boys that were exploiting his own daughter, in his very own home, while he was away at work trying to make a living for his family.

After hearing the truth about this precious young lady, something rose up inside of me. I call it "righteous indignation," and it kept turning my stomach upside down. It was an anger that required action, but I had no idea what to do. After all, the teenage boys had not broken any school board policy for which they could have been suspended. They were not on school grounds during school hours. I wrestled with what to do the entire day before retiring for the evening. I was carrying a very heavy heart with the burden for this straight "A" student and the entire family. I prayed myself to sleep and asked God to help me know what to do.

At 2:00 a.m. I awoke, got out of bed, went to the kitchen table and had an urge to start writing. When I was a teenager, I would write poems whenever I was upset. After finishing a poem, I would always feel better. I guess it was a kind of therapy that never failed to help my mood improve. This particular morning, I was not supposed to write a poem; I was supposed to write what God was getting ready to give to me.

By 5:00 a.m., I had finished what the Lord had given me for that day. For the next four nights in a row, the Holy Spirit woke me up at 2:00 a.m. sharp and had me write more of the vision for Project SOS until 5:00 a.m. I thought I would be exhausted, having lost so much sleep for those five long nights, but God gave me supernatural energy. I had never in my entire life felt more rested or energized!

By the end of the fifth night, I had been given the entire plan for beginning a not-for-profit organization that would eventually help teenagers be able to resist temptation, use refusal skills effectively, set boundaries, know the truth about STDs and pregnancies, avoid unhealthy relationships, and report abuse, molestation, and rape. Teens would be taught to write their goals and focus on those instead of sex, drugs, and alcohol. They would be able to discern the media messages that encourage them to have sex. Best of all they would open lines of communication with their parents. It was all right there, given to me by divine intervention.

I had never done something like this. I was neither prepared nor brave enough to say, "Oh, God, thank You so much for giving me my destiny! I can't wait to get started!" No, in fact, it was not something I even wanted to do. I spoke very frankly to God and said, "You know God, this is not in my plans. I want to run for a higher office. I really want to eventually go to Washington D.C. and represent the entire state of Florida." He didn't respond. I continued this one-way dialogue: "God, I really like being liked by other people. If I start talking to people about sex, they are not going to like me!" Again, God was silent. Then I started to rationalize why I couldn't possibly do what He was calling me to do: "Lord my plate is so full with chairing the school board, being a mother to two preteens, keeping the house nice and cooking the meals for my family. I can't possibly do one more thing!!! Oh, and by the way, if you haven't noticed God, I am only one person!" Then He broke His silence and the Holy Spirit reminded me of a verse in the Bible that says, "I will never leave you nor forsake you." He continued to speak to my heart, reminding me He had given me the names of the board members for Project SOS that I was to contact. I had run out of excuses. I was destined to do things God's way, not mine, and I am so glad I did. What I didn't know was that when God calls you to do something, He has already prepared others to help you. He goes before you and opens doors that no man can close. He gives you the gifts and talents you will need to do the job, usually through other Christians. He blesses you every step of the way and He gives you favor wherever you go.

So in 1993, I accepted the challenge God had given to me at my kitchen table in the middle of the night. We started with one classroom, in one school, with a budget of $68.00. For five years we were an all-volunteer organization. After 12 years we had reached over 200,000 teenagers and their parents. We had helped reduce the teen birth rates of 15-17 year old girls by 55%! Our health programs and mentoring clubs were in middle schools and high schools throughout six counties. We had trained people in cities throughout Russia to use the Project SOS model and trained thousands of abstinence educators to replicate what we were doing throughout the United States. In addition, we had produced a video series and marketed our products and services nationwide. I say all this not to brag, but to encourage you that when God calls you to do something for Him, don't hesitate. DO IT! Your Life will never be the same, nor will the lives of those He has called you to touch. Now enjoy reading about the lives of twelve of the people God brought to Project SOS. May God start to unfold your destiny as you read these true stories. Let me know how these stories have inspired you.

# YOU SEE

You see the finished product, but you could not conceive;

All my loving Father's led me
through to bring me to believe…

It is a process…sometimes arduous and long,

Sometimes joyful beyond words,
producing thankful songs…

View each story as a very special testimony of the
Father's perfect plan,

Motivated by His love…

I urge you from the start; please
do not compare our stories…

For your life is your gift to share.

And He has a different road you were designed to trod…

To lead you to a very special intimacy with our God.

We are to encourage one another while it is still today.

For the Father knew that this is
not an easy way that we're to travel…

The cost is truly great.

Ah… but for those who will endure we cannot anticipate

All He has in store for His very own;

So now, yours becomes a very special story through
which His love is shown…

Katherine Denham Osgood

# UGLY DUCKLING NO MORE!

An African American girl was born in North Florida into a family of four daughters, a hard-working father who started out driving a truck, and a VERY strict mother. Her name was Janette, and in her own words she says, "I felt so ugly growing up. I was tall, lanky, and hated everything about myself. My mother was very strict but I knew she loved me. By the time I was fifteen, I thought I should be able to make my own decisions. I'd say, 'Momma, can I go to....?' She would say, 'NO!' I'd say, 'Momma, don't you trust me?' She would say____? You guessed it, 'NO!' Actually when she was being really sweet, she would say, 'It's not that I don't trust you. I don't trust your friends!' That would really make me mad! I would get so mad that I would lock myself in my room and not talk to anyone for hours. Many mornings I would lock myself in the bathroom so I wouldn't have to go to school, because I didn't feel like I was good enough or smart enough or pretty enough. My momma would try to tell me that I was beautiful and that everything was okay, but until I was able to believe it for myself, I couldn't receive it from others, not even my momma. I thought of myself as the Ugly Ducking who would forever remain that way."

"My mom told me I would go to college someday and be somebody. I didn't feel like I could do much of anything, because I didn't have the confidence that my momma had in me. Because of her encouragement, I enrolled in college after high school. During the first week of my freshman year, I had to write a paper in one of my classes. I tried my hardest, but when I got the paper back, it was all marked in red ink. The professor told me that I was writing on a seventh grade level and that I didn't belong in college. I knew he was right, but guess what my Mother said when I told her I wanted to quit college because it was too hard and I couldn't do it? You guessed it again! That's right, she said, 'NO!' But this time she followed up her 'NO' word with words of encouragement by telling me that I could do it. She said I was smart enough, but that I needed to practice writing and persevere. My momma believed in me even when I didn't believe in myself."

"Remember, someone believes in you, too. Four years later, I could see my proud parents smiling as they saw their own daughter receive her diploma from the University of North Florida. My degree is in Logistics, something I was probably drawn to because of my father's transportation company. The funniest part is that I am not working in Logistics, but I am mentoring teenagers in over ten middle and high schools, including our regional detention center."

"I now get to tell teenagers that when my momma said, 'NO!' she wasn't trying to keep me "from" something. No, not at all; she was trying to keep me "for" something. Because of my parents, I can proudly say that I am still a virgin and have never done drugs or been drunk. I am thankful for my momma who only wanted the best for me. Because she set strict rules and boundaries, I am the person that I have become. I'm glad I listened to my momma. I now know that Mom has always been there for me. I thank her daily for making me into the woman I am today."

"I know someday (hopefully sooner than later) I will walk down the aisle of my church in a beautiful white wedding gown to give my entire body and soul (mind, emotions, and will) to the one man of my dreams. That will be the greatest day of my life! I'm proud to say I am also saving my first kiss for him!"

"By the way, I'm no longer that ugly duckling I once thought I was. I am tall, dark, and beautiful inside and out. God has given me a destiny to help teenagers understand that life does get easier as we grow older, and that strict parents really do love us. I enjoy encouraging teens to fulfill their destiny, regardless of past mistakes. I teach them how to kick down the walls of defeat through perseverance and not quitting. Walls may look insurmountable, but they are not. Our walls are there to teach us to be conquerors. They're not there to overcome us."

**Author's notes:** As I wrote Janette's story, I was reminded that as teenagers we ALL feel insecure and ugly most of the time. Rest assured that this is a normal stage of development in your life. Even the most admired, good-looking teens don't feel like they are worth much. Understand that if you guard your heart when you are young, you will then have a whole heart to present on your wedding night to your future spouse. The greatest gift you possess is your virginity. Your fiancé will appreciate your body being pure more than diamonds, money, or anything you can buy him or her. If you have unwrapped that gift, consider today rewrapping it and keeping it wrapped until your wedding night. It will be the best decision you will ever make. Your mate will be so proud of you when you walk down the aisle together and share your entire body with him or her on your wedding night. What a great exchange that will be!

## Lessons learned:

- Parents do the best job they can and truly do want you to succeed.
- Parents do know more than teenagers do, even if it doesn't seem like it at the time.
- Puberty is the hardest time of a person's life, but it will get easier as you grow older and mature out of the emotional roller coaster caused by hormonal changes during the teen years.
- Saving sex for marriage is a decision you will never regret.
- We all go through an ugly stage in life, but thank God it's only temporary.

## Scripture verses to learn:

- We also glory in tribulations, knowing that tribulation produces perseverance; and perseverance, character; and character, hope (Romans 5:3-4).
- Honor your father and your mother that your days may be long upon the land which the Lord your God is giving you (Exodus 20:12).

- Train up a child in the way he should go, and when he is old he will not depart from it (Proverbs 22:6).
- The rod and rebuke give wisdom, but a child left to himself brings shame to his mother (Proverbs 29:15).

# FROM GANG LEADER TO GREAT LEADER

Tim was the last born into a family of six children. Tim's father had a drinking problem, but his mother was a devout catholic. As Tim's father started drinking more, the violence escalated in his home. Tim hoped his father loved him, but his dad had no idea how to show affection. Tim hated his dad's drinking because he knew that fights would soon happen and, as an eight-year-old child, he couldn't protect his mother. He wanted to, but was powerless because of his size. Tim had seen more fighting, hitting, and yelling than any child should have endured. Before Tim was age nine, his dad returned to the reservation where he had grown up, and Tim would rarely see his father again after that time.

In one sense, Tim was happy his father was gone, because the drinking, fighting, and yelling were gone also, but on the other hand, Tim loved his father as all boys do and wondered when and if he would return again. Tim missed his father being at home. Deep down inside, he felt like he had been abandoned. That feeling caused him great fear. After all, who was going to look after the family? Tim was too small, but he really wanted to lead and show that he could be a man, even at the tender age of eight. Tim wanted to be all grown up so he covered his deep feelings of fear by putting on the tough guy act, building a wall of protection around his heart. He secretly promised himself that no one would ever penetrate that wall. That way he would never be hurt again.

While Tim's mother was trying to cope with getting a divorce and taking care of six children, Tim was looking for attention. He found that if he did something wrong, then everyone would notice him and give him the attention he craved. He was also looking to fit in with older guys, hoping to be like a man and stop feeling like the boy he truly was. He found that the older boys in the neighborhood would let him join them as long as he would go along with whatever they were doing to entertain themselves until their mothers returned from work. He noticed that none of them had fathers at home either. In fact, a lot of them didn't even know who their fathers were.

By age ten Tim had followed the older boys into a habit of smoking cigarettes and drinking at the park. Most of them had dropped out of school, so by the time he was in the fifth grade, Tim started ditching school more often than he attended. Soon, he was so far behind in his schoolwork that he just stopped going to school altogether. After all, in comparison to his worldly experiences, his classmates seemed like babies. His mother would plead with him to go to school, but he would just walk out the door and leave for several days until things calmed down. Then he would reappear, take a shower, get some clean clothes and eat some home-cooked food until the next reason to leave.

The biggest day of Tim's life was when his older buddies asked him if he wanted to become a full-fledged brother in their neighborhood gang. Tim felt like he was finally accepted. He had found the approval he so desperately sought from his father. He had everything a fatherless boy needed: an identity with a group known for being tough and a support system that would watch his back and keep him safe from the law. Tim finally felt like the man he knew he wanted to become.

By age eleven Tim had been introduced to his first joint. The feeling he had after that first high was numbness, a mask that would cover his deep feelings of fear and pain. That numbness would become Tim's escape from the reality of his true pain and the guilt feelings caused by the way he was treating his mother and his family.

At age twelve Tim lost his virginity, and that same year, on a dare, he committed his first real crime. Feeling accepted by the older teenagers was not enough for Tim. He set a goal: to become the youngest leader of the neighborhood mafia. He knew he would have to show his buddies how tough he was, so he worked out during the day and started to develop muscles. At night he would "hang out" with his gang members drinking, trying different drugs, and robbing houses and cars. Tim was living a lifestyle way beyond his control, but he knew he couldn't turn back, especially if he wanted to be their leader.

By the time Tim was thirteen, he was a repeat offender and knew most of the names of the staff at the local detention center. He enjoyed his frequent stays there, because the staff guards were big men who really came down hard on him, but at the same time, he felt that they truly cared about him. They had strict rules and guidelines, and Tim actually thrived in that military atmosphere. Tim's future looked pretty predictable: He would either be locked up in prison for a gun-related crime or he would be killed by rival gang members. Either way, he didn't care as long as someone noticed him. His life had turned into either one big whirlwind of adrenaline rush while living out his gang life, or deep valleys of depression caused by withdrawal from drugs and alcohol after being arrested and locked up.

One thing Tim remembered about his trips to the detention center was a special guard who worked the night shift. This man was a huge African-American who seemed to take a liking to him. After he was in his bunk, this guard would go in to see Tim in his cellblock. Tim would pretend he was sleeping, but remembered everything that guard did and said. That large man quietly tiptoed up to Tim's bunk, laid his hands on Tim's chest, and prayed over him. Tim remembered the words he would pray each night: "Dear heavenly Father, I pray that you would forgive this young man. I pray that you would turn his life around and use it for your good. Bring someone into his life that can help him to change and be a leader for good instead of evil. In Jesus' name I pray, Amen." Tim knew that the guard saw something in him others couldn't see, not even himself. He wanted someone to recognize his potential. He wanted more for his life than what the gang had to offer, but felt totally helpless to change his future. After all, who would want to hire a fifth-grade drop-out with an extensive criminal record?

On Tim's fourteenth birthday he was released from one of his many stays at the local detention center. His mother was a friend of mine. The day Tim was released, I called his mom to see if her daughter could speak at a school the next day. I needed a volunteer available to go talk to teenagers about making healthy choices. Tim's mother told me her daughter was working. She went on to tell me about her son's life and said he was available if I wanted to take the chance. Something deep inside of me said, "Take a chance. You need a teenager and he's the only one available. Don't worry."

That night at the family table I tried to calmly mention to my husband and two teenage sons that I was picking up a young man named Tim who had just been released from the detention center and that he would speak at my program the next morning. My husband, David, being the cautious, protective man that he is, looked up from his plate of spaghetti and said, "You're doing what tomorrow?" I knew if David found out all the facts about Tim's life, he would forbid me to go, so I kept the sordid details to myself. My oldest son, Jon, age fifteen, said nothing except, "Pass me some more garlic bread, please." Our youngest son, Justin, thirteen, asked, "Where does he go to school, and why does he get to skip to go with you and we can't?" Our sons were used to hearing my stories about my volunteers, but they had never heard a story like Tim's. I told Justin that Tim wasn't in school. Unfortunately, Justin's mind was racing with questions and asked, "Well, how old is he?" When I said fourteen, both of our boys looked up at me from their half-eaten plates of food and said at the same time, "That's not fair! Why do we have to go to school if he doesn't?" I tried to give the briefest answer I could. "He's been in some trouble and so he dropped out of school." I could feel the stares coming from my husband. I knew what the next question would be, and my hunch was confirmed when all three of them said, "What kind of trouble?" As I gave a short version of the long laundry list of Tim's charges, one of our sons said, "Mom, promise us one thing." I said "Maybe," thinking they were going to be protective of their mother and not want me to pick up Tim to go with me. Instead, the boys said at the same time, "Whatever you do, don't take dad's new car tomorrow!" So much for protecting their mother!

The next morning, the volunteer nurse with Project SOS, Emily Campbell, and I picked up Tim at 6:00 a.m.. As he departed from his mother's van and opened the door to my seven-year-old vehicle, I could see his starched white shirt and khaki pants. As he took his seat next to me, I was amazed that he was only fourteen. He had bulging muscles and a well-established mustache. On his left hand he had gang tattoos, but his long-sleeved shirt covered the other ones that he would proudly show me later.

We learned a great deal about Tim on that hour ride to the school. His last arrest was for stealing a car. I tried not to look worried as I said, "Well, no one would want this old thing. It has over 100,000 miles on it and doesn't run real well either. In fact, it's a miracle that we haven't broken down yet!" Tim assured me he wasn't the least bit interested in my vehicle, because in his words it was an "old lady car." That was the first time in my forty years of age I had ever been glad to be thought of as an old lady!

After an hour and a half drive, we pulled up to the middle school where we would present our program about abstinence from sex, drugs, alcohol, crime, and violence to four hundred eighth graders. Before exiting the car, Tim mentioned his mouth was really dry. I later learned that one sign of fear is a dry mouth, but he never let us know how he truly felt. Actually, I was the one in sheer panic, and I could tell by Emily's face that she wasn't feeling much better.

Following the graphic slide presentation about sexually transmitted diseases, I introduced Tim to the rambunctious group of thirteen-year-olds. As he walked onto the cafeteria stage and looked into the eyes of the four hundred teenagers, everyone, including Tim, became silent. After what seemed to be forever, Tim opened his mouth and spoke reality into the lives of those very privileged, sheltered teenagers. He spoke with great authority and commanded respect from each and every student. The room was totally silent as he shared his personal testimony about the poor choices he had made in his life. He talked about the sex, drugs, alcohol, gang life and the consequences of being arrested. He told them about only having a fifth grade education and how it made him feel insecure and uneducated. He talked about having no future and no decent friends like they had in their lives. He shared his heart with those teens and then said, "Don't make the same mistakes I have made so you won't ruin your life like I have done." He continued, "I have no future; you do. Avoid the choices I made and be thankful for your life and the opportunities you still have." He concluded by showing the audience the rosary beads his mother had given him and said, "Pray to God and he'll get you through anything."

As Tim stepped down from the stage, the teens clapped so loudly the room seemed to shake. Then they rose to their feet in cheers for him. Tim never smiled, not even one time, but I could tell by his body language that he was shocked at the outpouring of adoration being shown to him. At the same time he was relieved to be off the stage, but also grateful for their response. Emily and I knew that very moment that Tim had just finished doing what God intended him to do: use his life to help others do better than he had done.

For the rest of that school year, Tim probably spoke to 2,000 teenagers about his life and the consequences of the unhealthy choices he had made. Every speech he made had a tremendous impact on all of the teenagers' lives. Before each talk, his mouth was always dry. After a few months of talking, I started to see a smiling, happy young man emerge from the hard, tough guy he had been. Tim had found his destiny, his purpose and the calling God had for his life. He had become a leader for good and actually didn't have as much time left to hang out with his former gang members. Unfortunately, when he did have time to be with them, he would revert from being a leader for good to being his old self, the neighborhood mafia gang leader. There was truly a battle raging inside of him, a battle of good versus evil.

After Tim worked for me for several months, I realized he had no idea what an intact, reasonably healthy family looked like. That's when I had an amazing brainstorm. Now, rest assured, my boys and husband were used to my brainstorms and would usually say "no" before I could even finish telling them my idea. They knew every one of my brainstorms cost them something in time, money, or talents, and this one was no exception. I announced one bright, sunny morning during breakfast that we needed to invite Tim to spend the next weekend with us so he could feel like part of a family that had a mother and father who loved each other. I wanted Tim to be able to observe an intact family, warts and all! As expected, they were anything but overjoyed. They also knew if the only female in the family didn't get her way, life would be pretty miserable for several days. (We mothers do have our ways of getting what we know everyone needs. It is true, when Momma's not happy, then nobody's happy! Some of our secrets are withholding food or drink, losing the remote control, becoming very quiet, only giving one-word answers, slamming cupboards, or when forced to, we can have an old fashioned fit, better than any two-year-old can do!) After trying all of the above, my guys said, "Okay, Tim can come over for the weekend, but we'll have to lock up any valuables, especially our hunting guns!"

After driving forty-five minutes across town to his house, I picked Tim up and we drove back to my home. He was unusually quiet in the car, so I asked him if his mouth was dry. He said "yes." I pulled into a fast food place and bought two Cokes. I knew he was fearful and could certainly understand why. Going to my house for the weekend meant meeting our two teenage sons and their father, which meant facing possible rejection or maybe worse. As we sat drinking our Cokes, I told Tim that our boys were really looking forward to meeting him and hanging out. He tried to smile in order to hide his true fear.

As we drove into my neighborhood, I could tell he had never been in a gated community before, at least not legally in the daylight! He was in awe of the manicured yards, cars parked in garages instead of on the grass, and chimneys with actual smoke coming out of them like you see in Christmas pictures. I must confess that I felt a little uneasy when Tim admired one of my neighbor's new SUVs.

As we pulled into the driveway, all three of the Mullarkey guys were standing outside waiting for Tim. I looked at him and said, "It's going to be okay," as he clinched the door handle, took a deep breath, and opened the car door. When he stepped out from the "old lady" vehicle, the reception was like a man coming home from battle. He was met with handshakes, smiles, and the casual jokes that our youngest son was so well-known for cracking. Tim gave one of his rare smiles and went off with our sons into their rooms to entertain themselves by playing video games, wrestling and doing whatever teenagers do.

It was one weekend none of us will ever forget, especially Tim. He was a perfect gentleman, just as his mother had raised him to be. I was so proud of our two sons, who included Tim in all of their activities with their gang of friends: fishing in the back yard, wearing camouflage in the canoe, playing with the dogs, driving around Ponte Vedra Beach showing Tim some of the homes, and just hanging out together. We sat down as a family during dinner both Friday and Saturday nights and Tim seemed to really enjoy laughing and talking together over my home-cooked meals. It was just as though Tim had always been a part of our family, just another one of the Mullarkey boys! Our home was always filled with several other boys that would come over to play video games or just chill out together. This weekend, with Tim, was no exception.

One thing all of us noticed about Tim on that first weekend was that he scrutinized every move that David, my husband, made. After noticing this at the dinner table on Friday night, I told David, "You'd better be on your best behavior 'cause Tim is watching every move you make." David grinned and said, "He can take me or leave me. I am who I am, and I'm not going to change for anyone, especially a fourteen-year-old kid." That was the way David always was. What you saw was who he was, no pretending, no front, nothing but the real thing, take it or leave it.

On Sunday morning we went together as a family to church and Tim came with us. He had never been in a church that wasn't Catholic. Our church was very different from what he had experienced before in church. There was no beautiful church building, altar or pews, no prayer books, no priest dressed in robes, nor any rote prayers that everyone recited together. Instead, there was singing, dancing, and overflowing joy coming from the people sitting in hard-backed chairs in a very unpretentious gymnasium. The pastor, Steve McCoy, was a big man who stood over six feet tall, and when he spoke, it was as if the words were coming from a gentle giant. They were words of healing, grace, and mercy about a loving God who would forgive even the worst of sinners. Pastor Steve knew what he was talking about, because he once lived a lifestyle filled with drugs, fighting, hate, and anger. God had changed his heart, replacing those things with love for the down and out and with an understanding of the tremendous need people have for God's mercy, grace, unconditional love, and forgiveness. To this day Beaches Chapel is like a healing hospital that ministers to those who are the broken victims of life's cruel experiences.

As we walked in the door of the gymnasium that serves as our house of worship, many people came up to Tim and hugged him and welcomed him as a brother in the Lord. After we found our seats in the front of the gym, the band cranked up their praise and worship songs. We all stood to our feet and began clapping and moving to the beat while little children came rushing to the stage to dance together to the music, praising God for all of His blessings. You could see some adults playing tambourines and once in a while, you would hear some-one yell out a shout of thanksgiving to the Lord. As the music became slower, the children returned to their seats next to their parents, and the entire congregation, still standing, worshipped the Lord with all of their hearts. Some had their hands in the air in total abandonment; some knelt on the hard gym floor while others stood singing with their eyes closed. Many wept with joy of how their lives were being restored and their emotions being tenderized once again after years of being numbed with drugs, pain or the scars from life's experiences. They sang songs about the forgiveness of God for all of their past mistakes and of this new relationship they had found through the love of Jesus Christ. As the praise and worship continued, I looked over at Tim, and for the first time I saw a tear fall from his eyes as he was observing and basking in the presence of what could only be described as the Holy Spirit. I could tell that the Lord was moving on Tim's heart, chiseling away at the wall that had been built by pain, rejection, abandonment, and fear.

After hearing Pastor Steve's message, Tim leaned over to me and whispered, "He really knows how we feel, doesn't he?" I said, "Yes, he knows better than most how Christ can change a heart of stone to a heart of love." I believe that morning was the beginning of an awakening in Tim's spirit that would draw him into a very personal, close relationship with his Creator, the same Creator of the universe. Tim had been to church for many years with his mom, brothers and sisters, but that day God was giving him a knock on the door of his heart that every "born again" Christian can never forget. When we arrived home from church, we ate lunch together and then the boys went outside. We were all a little bit quiet at lunch because we knew that Tim would soon be leaving. At 4:00, I told him I would need to drive him home, so he gathered his things and met me in the kitchen where David was waiting. As we were all saying our goodbyes, my husband took Tim's handshake and drew him into his chest and gave him one of his gentle bear hugs and said, "I love you, Tim." As he did, Tim stiffened up, turned his head, took his duffle bag and went directly to the "old lady" car. I looked at David and the boys with surprise. They smiled at me with understanding that only males could share.

He never made eye contact with me for the entire forty-five minute drive, nor did he say a word. He looked out the window the whole time. I could see from the reflection in his window that he was wiping his eyes from the tears he was not able to control. I didn't try to make conversation with Tim, knowing words were not needed. I knew that God was dealing with his heart and that I needed to stay out of the way. As I drove into his grass driveway, I turned off the engine and asked Tim if he was okay. He said, "Yes, Miss Pam, but can I ask you a question?" I said, "Of course you can, Tim. I'll tell you anything you want to know." As he sniffed and wiped a tear from his eye, he looked straight into my eyes and asked, "Is Mr. Mullarkey gay?" In my total astonishment, I told him, "Of course not!" I asked him what would make him even think to ask that question. Tim's reply was one of the greatest revelations I'd ever heard. He said, "Well, I saw Mr. Mullarkey hugging Jon and Justin and telling them he loved them. Then when I was leaving, he hugged me and told me he loved me." I said, "Tim, that's what a father does. What did you think a father was supposed to do?" Tim, still looking into my eyes to see if I was telling the truth, said with all honesty, "I thought the only time a man was supposed to touch a boy was when he was beating him, unless he was gay, of course." When those words came out of his mouth, I realized Tim had so much to learn about being a man and a father. I also knew his first weekend at our house would be one of many to come.

All the way home from Tim's house, I prayed for him. I thanked God that we were allowed to sow some seeds of truth into this young man's life and that he would be learning many new revelations, especially about what a true man was supposed to act like. As I was driving and praying, God brought back a memory to me. Before I had visited David's home, I thought that all married couples yelled and screamed at each other every day. Upon my first visit to his house, I found that my narrow idea of marriage was not the norm. His parents were laughing and talking together with their three sons. I had never seen anything like it, but I knew that I longed for that kind of marriage. Likewise, Tim needed to visit our home to see how a healthy father interacts with his children.

For the next three years, Tim grew up in so many ways. He was a regular monthly visitor in our home, and every time he was a perfect gentleman. Tim knew how to behave and have a good time, making healthy choices when he was away from the negative pressure of his mafia friends. When he would return home and hang out with his homeboys, he would get arrested again. Finally, the juvenile judge, Judge Crenshaw, placed him in a drug treatment center where he learned to face the pain of his past and begin to find freedom from the addictions that covered his memories. At one point the pain of the memories was so intense that Tim decided to run away from the drug rehab center. As he went to step off the property to freedom from dealing with his issues, three police cars drove past him. That's when God spoke to his heart for the first time and said, "Tim, I sent these three cars to represent the trinity of the Father, Son, and Holy Spirit. I will be with you through all of the pain. With Me, you will conquer your fears. Turn around, go back in, and face your demons head on. Together we can overcome anything." That very moment was the greatest turning point in Tim's life. If he had stepped off the property, he would have been rearrested and sent to the adult prison system that the judge promised. Instead, he slowly turned around, returned to his bed and felt a deep peace that he had never felt before. He knew that night that he would never be alone again and that he could trust God with everything, even his horrible childhood memories.

Several months later, right before Tim's graduation from the drug treatment center, he was allowed to leave and stay with us for a weekend. This time we all knew that he was truly changed. He was clean, sober, and his heart was very tender. His hard outer shell had been pierced and the love and life of a new, free man had emerged. As the Bible says, Tim was a new creation in Christ Jesus, and all the old had gone and the new had come.

After graduation from the treatment center, Tim went back to his mother's house, but instead of joining his former gang members, he tried to help them change their lives like he had. They were not one bit interested in becoming like Tim and, in fact, they told him to get out of their lives if he wasn't willing to continue the life of sex, drugs, alcohol, and crime. Tim walked away from them feeling like a failure because he hadn't been able to lead them away from their gang life and all that went along with that kind of living. I believe that day Tim truly became a man. He had learned one of the hardest lessons he would ever learn in life, which is that we can only change one person: ourselves.

Tim came to our house for several weeks until an apartment came open through the juvenile offender's program. Tim would speak for Project SOS during the day and work painting our house in the evenings. This was the first paying job he had ever had and the first legal money he had ever earned. He was a very hard worker and I would paint alongside of him, which gave us time to talk on a personal level. He would always ask deep questions about life that we could sort out together. One very hot day while Tim was painting, he took off his shirt. To my surprise, there were large red scars that were in the same place where his gang tattoos once were. I asked him about them and he said that he had them cut away so he would have nothing left of his former gang lifestyle. He said that because he never wanted to take drugs again, he didn't allow the doctor to give him any pain medication before cutting them out with a knife. The scars were large and covered his arms, hands and chest. Ridges of bright red tissue were forming that made them stick out very noticeably. I couldn't help but imagine the horrible pain Tim must have experienced with no pain medication before, during, or after the operation. Then I was reminded of the more painful memories and scars that he must have had from a lifestyle that robbed his goals, dreams and, ultimately, his childhood.

One day the much-awaited news came. Tim's mother called and said, "Son, your apartment is ready. Come on home and we'll pack up your things so you can start your new life." With the juvenile system of the state of Florida wanting to reestablish former delinquents into housing and jobs, Tim was given an apartment and he was even hired for a job at the local Wal-Mart. Our sons were quite green with envy that Tim, who was only seventeen, could have an apartment of his own, while they had to live at home at ages 16 and 18 and have parents checking to see that their homework was done so they would graduate from high school. That hardly seemed fair to them.

Before Tim walked to my "old lady" car to go back home to pack up for his new start, he ran up to my husband David and gave him the biggest bear hug he could give. Then he said out loud, "I love you, dad! Thanks for everything you've done for me. I'll always be grateful. You have no idea what your family has meant to me." My husband hugged him back, told him he loved him, and gave him a word of advice, "Tim, don't forget; stay away from the other side of town, okay." He said yes, hugged everyone else, put his stuff in my car, and yelled out the car window, "I'll see you soon." I drove him home for the last time to start his new and exciting life!

Our family talked to Tim several times in the next few weeks. He was so proud of his Wal-Mart badge he wore to work. He was getting ready to start a GED course at the local community college within walking distance from his apartment. He was doing great and we were so proud of him. After all, we felt like he was one of our own sons. He had been totally abstinent from sex, drugs, alcohol, violence, and crime for seventeen months, and his future looked brighter than ever before. He was full of hope and had an excitement in his voice I had not heard before. He was now too busy at his new job and attending school to speak for Project SOS, but promised to still talk to the boys at the local detention center on Saturday afternoons when his job permitted. As a former inmate himself, when he spoke, everybody listened. He had a tremendous effect on those juvenile offenders. He would get right up in their faces and say to them, "You are so cool, aren't you? Just look how tough you are now sitting with someone else's jumpsuit on, wearing someone else's dirty shoes, sleeping in a strange bed, being told when you can go to the can, when you can eat, and what you can and cannot do. You really are cool aren't you?" He would continue, "I've been in those same clothes. I've slept in your bed many times and I've done more crime, drugs, alcohol and sex than any of you in here. I'm here to tell you that you are NOT COOL, you're NOT BAD, and you have NO future! You are nothing but a punk, and right now you are a total loser! I know because I used to be one too. Now because of the choices I've made and the people I've allowed to help me get out of my former gang life, I am cool! Now I really am somebody! I have a job, a girlfriend, and an apartment. Now I'm a real man because I am making responsible choices. Unless you are willing to make a change in your life today, you'll be back here over and over again. If I can do it, anyone can!" Then Tim would stay and mentor with the ones who wanted to change their lifestyles. Tim was giving back from appreciation of all he had received. The results were amazing. Hundreds of young men allowed Tim to minister to them. Tim was truly fulfilling his God-given destiny. God's Word was coming to pass where in the book of Joel God says, "I will restore the years that the locusts have eaten." God also said, "I will bring you out with rejoicing and peace in your hearts."

One day, not long after Tim had started his new and better life, his mother called me and said, "Pam, are you sitting down?" I sat down and said, "Yes, what is it?" She said the most painful words I could have heard, "Pam, Tim is dead!" I screamed, "No! He can't be dead! He's got his life together. He's finally happy and settled down and doing so great. Tell me it's not true!" She said, "I wish I could tell you that I made it up, but the truth is Tim is dead." She explained that he had gotten a ride with a friend who had a pickup truck. They were driving too fast in the rain and the wind caught up under the flatbed and picked the truck up in the air. The sixteen-year-old driver over responded, cutting the wheel really sharply which caused the truck to slam into a concrete telephone pole. Both boys were killed instantly upon impact. She went on to say that no drugs or alcohol were found or involved in the accident. I was grateful for that, but devastated that Tim had been killed. I asked her one question, "What side of town were they driving on?" She answered that they were just entering her side when the accident happened." As I hung up the phone, I told David what had happened. When he found out Tim was on the other side of town, he slammed his fist on the countertop in rage and yelled, "I told him to stay away from that side of the city! Why didn't he listen to me? I knew something like this was going to happen if he returned to that side of town!" We then grabbed each other, hugged and cried until the boys came home from their sports activities. When they walked in the door, they knew something tragic had happened, but they never imagined that Tim would be dead.

For the first time in my short time of being a true believer in Christ, I was really angry with God. I went to the beach and cried and walked and even yelled at God saying, "How could you have allowed Tim to be killed at seventeen years of age? He had so much to live for! His life was finally on track and he was like a son to us. How could you have let this happen?" I even tried to reason with God that Tim was the only person I had that could truly reach the hearts of juvenile delinquents, but God was silent. I couldn't seem to feel His presence. My anger at God would soon turn to feelings of grief and depression as my family and I went to Tim's funeral. The church was full of mourners, some family friends, some church friends, and even some people whose lives had been changed by Tim's testimony that he gave with Project SOS at schools, detention centers, and churches. As I sat there looking at the people, I wondered why the front rows of pews were empty, yet the rest of the church was completely full. I didn't know who the seats were saved for, but God had reserved them for a very special moment in the lives of some very special young men. Right before the service began, in walked over a hundred guys, their pants bagged down below their butts and shinny chains swung as they strolled down the aisle. The only available seats in the church were in front. I could tell from the smell that they had been smoking pot before walking into the service. I assumed that most of them had never set foot into a church before attending the funeral service of their former gang leader.

Fortunately for Tim's family, the Catholic bishops were in town for a conference and they decided to officiate the funeral service. As one of the elderly bishops rose to his feet and slowly walked to the microphone, every eye was on him, including each of the gang members. As he spoke, he gave a clear gospel message about the love of Christ and how He took away our sins through the shedding of His blood on the cross. He said His blood washed away our sin and we were given forgiveness through His sacrificial death.

The second speaker, and last to address the audience with a eulogy about Tim's life, was Judge Mack Crenshaw, Juvenile Judge for the county where the gang was established. As this tall statue of a man rose to the microphone, he acknowledged several of the gang members on the front row by their first names. He had seen all of them numerous times in his court, much like he had seen Tim until Tim's life was changed. Judge Crenshaw spoke about the change that had taken place in Tim's life and how Christ could come into anyone's life and make that same difference. He spoke of how God could take the garbage out of a person's life and grind it up and use it as a fertilizer for someone else's good to grow them closer to Him. As he spoke about the heart change that Christ had performed on Tim, something started to happen to the hearts of these tough gang members. Something powerful was reaching down into those boys' hearts of stone, grinding them and polishing them as only God can do in order to turn us into beautiful gems. As the Judge continued to speak about how Christ changed the desires of Tim's heart, which changed his actions, the Holy Spirit fell on those front row seats. Every boy started to weep and those cries turned into sobs. Most of these boys had not allowed themselves to cry in years, but God was piercing their hearts as the Judge showed them the unconditional love of their heavenly Father. As he continued to speak, I could see that their tears were tears of regret that they hadn't listened to Tim when he had come back to them to try to get them to change their lives. Now that Tim was dead, they were able to hear what he had been trying to say. None of these boys knew about a father's love. Most of them didn't even know who their fathers were, much less whom their heavenly Father was. Not even the toughest efforts were able to hold back the tears of pain that these gang members were experiencing that very special afternoon as God selected the entire group to introduce Himself to for the first time.

When the funeral ended, and as most of the people in the church filed out to go to the cemetery, it started to rain. The gang members stayed in their seats and waited until each one of them had received a hug from Judge Crenshaw. It was a father's hug that they had so desperately needed and wanted, but couldn't find until that very special funeral of their former gang leader. As I looked at their faces, I saw them as the little boys that they really were inside, all desiring someone to unconditionally love them and give them a purpose for their lives. As they arose in formation to leave the church, they all realized that they had been touched and changed forever by the power of an unseen, yet powerful God.

After the burial service, the local news channel had arranged to do a live microphone interview for anyone who wanted to speak about the loss of one of the city's most notorious former gang leaders. One by one, each of the gang members went to the microphone and spoke about how he planned to change his life because of Tim's death. They removed their gang symbols of clothing, piling them together so they could later take them to the site of Tim's fatal crash and leave them at the base of that concrete telephone pole as a sign of their changed lives.

That rainy afternoon, at a funeral service, over a hundred dangerous gang members turned their lives over to Christ and gave up their gang membership forever, never to be resurrected again. That neighborhood mafia had died along with our beloved son, Tim.

As I walked on the beach the next day, I had to ask God to forgive me for my narrow, unfaithful response to Tim's death. God forgave me as He does everyone who asks, but He also reminded me of the scripture that says, "My ways are not your ways. My thoughts are not your thoughts. My ways are higher than your ways." I thanked God for using Tim's death to bring his friends to salvation. As I opened the car door to leave the beach, the Holy Spirit gave me this scripture to remember whenever I thought about Tim: "There is no greater love than this: that a man lay down his life for his friends."

**Lessons learned:**

1. Everybody has a purpose and plan for their lives. No one knows how many years anyone is given to live. Make the best of the years you have been given by giving back to God. This is the secret of true happiness.
2. Salvation is a free gift. You can't earn it or deserve it. You receive it by faith in Jesus Christ.
3. No one has done so many bad things that our loving heavenly Father can't forgive, forget, and get him/her back on track serving others.
4. Hang out with friends that will make you a better person, not ones that will get you into trouble.
5. Know that God has a purpose for everything, even death. Trust Him, even when you don't understand why something has happened.

## Scriptures to learn:

- For by grace you have been saved through faith, and that not of yourselves; it is the gift of God, not of works, lest anyone should boast (Ephesians 2:8-9).
- And we know that all things work together for good to those who love God, to those who are the called according to His purposes (Romans 8:28).
- In Him (Jesus Christ) we have redemption through His blood, the forgiveness of sins, according to the riches of His grace which He made to abound toward us in all wisdom and prudence (Ephesians 1:7-8).
- Blessed are those whose lawless deeds are forgiven, and whose sins are covered. Blessed is the man to whom the Lord shall not impute sin (Romans 4:7-8).
- There is therefore now NO condemnation to those who are in Christ Jesus, who do not walk according to the flesh, but according to the spirit (Romans 8:1).
- Jesus said to her, I am the resurrection and the life. He who believes in me, though he may die, he shall live (John 11:25).

# THE MASTERPIECE

He eyes a great block of Granite and sees a masterpiece…

His focus…. Superhuman… all distractions cease…

The sculptor aptly chips away all that is in the way

Of the masterpiece he saw and wants so to display.

That's how the Heart of God is,
when He views the heart of man.

He falls in love with what
He sees then embarks upon a plan…

To chip away all the subterfuge
that should not be there…

And He creates His masterpiece
that He delights to share…

When the Father looked at you
despite what condition you were in

He did not see the garbage, the decay and the sin…

He looked through eyes of love and saw you differently,

The way that He created you,
and He set out to set you free.

Katherine Denham Osgood

# THE BIG TALK

Eric was the middle child, with two older brothers and two younger brothers. It seemed to Eric that everyone in the lineup was filled with talents except him. His brothers were gifted in music, drama, storytelling, communicating, sports, or anything else they tried to do. Eric felt rather insecure around all of his talented brothers, and on top of that, he was the smallest one in the family. He really felt like the black sheep that didn't belong. His father could see Eric was smaller than the others and not quite as gifted, so he spent extra time with him. They would hang out together, spend time on special projects, or they would just go to the store by themselves. He worshipped his father and wanted to grow up to be just like him. He felt special when they were together. Eric's best friend was his father, and his dad knew that and loved it.

Eric's father would take him to school everyday, even if the other brothers were riding the bus or catching rides with friends. He felt so proud when his dad would let him off at the front door of the school building and give him a big hug and tell him he would see him at home for dinner. Eric couldn't wait to see his dad every night. His life was great with no major problems, no girlfriends to worry about, and a great family and fun youth group he attended at church.

One morning Eric's father asked him to be ready for school a little early on that particular day. He rushed to brush his teeth, comb his hair and get his books packed up so he could be ready on time to please his father. He figured that they would probably go for a special breakfast or something different like that since they were leaving early. He was filled with excitement at the suspense of what the surprise would be.

Eric was a bit disappointed when his dad didn't offer him anything out of the ordinary that morning. He just said that they would get to school early so they could talk. Actually, that was okay with Eric because he treasured his man-to-man talks. It was special enough just to have quality time with his dad. He would ask his father all kinds of meaningful questions, like "Were you ever the smallest kid in your class?" Eric's dad would have just the right answer to encourage him, soothing his pain like a cool ointment spread on a sunburned shoulder.

As his dad drove him up to the front of the school building and found a parking space that was empty, he turned off the engine. Eric was anticipating this special talk-time because mornings were usually rushed with getting four boys ready for school and making sure everyone had their lunches and had brushed their teeth. This morning they would share quality time together, because his dad had cared enough to talk with him man to man. He didn't know what they were going to talk about, but he knew it wouldn't matter as long as they were together.

Eric noticed his dad had a hard time looking at him. He wondered if he had done something wrong and his father was getting ready to reprimand him. He scrolled through his memory banks to try and pull up the last thing he shouldn't have done. Did his dad know that he really hadn't been brushing his teeth in the mornings, but instead swishing with mouthwash? Maybe one of his teachers had called to report that he had not turned in his homework again. Eric knew that no matter what his dad said, they could work things out together, because they were known as a team. "Whatever you've done, we can always get through it together, Eric," he would periodically say.

This morning would be different, however. This talk would be one Eric and his father had never had, one that would change his life and family forever. His dad, looking at the gearshift, hesitantly spoke these chilling words, "Son, your mother and I are going to separate for a while, and I am moving out of the house tomorrow." Those words were like a cold knife driven right through his son's heart. He knew this meant divorce because he had seen other kids his age go through the same thing, but he never thought in his wildest imaginations that his father would ever say those heartbreaking words to him! Eric took one look at his father, opened the car door and ran into the school building. His dad tried to get him to stop and come back to the car to talk, but he didn't want to hear his father's voice ever again!

During homeroom, Eric didn't hear anything anyone said to him. He didn't even know the morning announcements had been on when the first-period bell rang. He could only wonder what was going to happen to his family and especially to him. After the bell rang, he felt like he was in a trance as he walked in slow motion to the locker room for gym class. Voices in the hallway were all muffled. They sounded like annoying barks from dogs that won't shut up when you're trying to sleep. Eric was going through the motions of walking, just putting one foot in front of the other. He didn't care where he was going or when he would get there. Finally he found himself standing in front of his locker as he reached the handle and opened the squeaky metal door. Only then did the reality of losing his dad, his very best friend in the whole world, hit him like he had been run over by a Mack truck racing down a dirt road at ninety miles an hour. The truth of what his dad had said began to sink into his heart and he started to cry like a baby. His emotions were over-whelming as the fear of his future gripped his heart. Crying uncontrollably, he tried to hide his face in his locker so the other kids wouldn't see him and make fun of him. He was in no mood to be teased. He usually had a great sense of humor when the other guys would say something to him about his size, but this morning was truly a different kind of day than he had ever experienced before.

The other guys in his gym class must have felt his pain and somehow knew that he needed to be alone. Without a word, they passed by his locker where they heard him crying and went on to gym class. After all, what could a boy say to another boy who was as hurt and upset as he was? Eric appreciated his friends leaving him alone so he could have time by himself in the locker room. As he stood with his head leaning against the locker door, questions raced through his mind: *How could my dad do this to me? What could he be thinking? What is mom going to do without dad? What will I do without my dad at home? Who will take me to school in the mornings? Who will I have to talk to now that dad is leaving? Do my brothers know yet and how will they react?* Suddenly his family meant more to him that he had ever realized.

Eric mustered up enough courage to walk to the main office after the last guy had dressed out and left the locker room. He took time to wash his face in an attempt to make it look like he hadn't been crying. He knew that it wasn't cool for men to cry, so he did his best to look down and not make eye contact with the lady at the front desk. He just asked her to call his mother so he could go home. As a mom, she sensed that Eric needed his mother more than ever on that particular day and at that particular time. She immediately called and asked her to come to school to pick up her son. She knew that Eric's dad had told him the news and she was waiting for the call from the school. When Eric's mom arrived, she could see that he had been crying and her heart felt so heavy and broken, but she knew words could not heal the emotions Eric was experiencing. After all, she was a broken woman trying to survive for her five children, not knowing what was in store for any of them. She remembered asking her husband not to tell their sons before school, but he insisted because he wanted to leave that very evening. Eric and his mom spent the entire afternoon crying together. That was the day he made a vow to himself. He would never, ever forgive his dad for the pain he had caused him and his family.

From then on, Eric would barely speak to his father. He was so hurt and angry that he couldn't even look him in the eyes whenever he was around. His dad tried everything, but Eric would have nothing to do with his former best friend.

Eric's church youth group leaders knew what he was going through and they worked every week mentoring

Eric and making him feel special like his dad had done. His favorite youth pastor took him to dinner one evening and shared some wisdom with him. He said, "Eric, everyone feels insecure, especially the showoffs and bullies. They feel the worst and that's why they act that way. Even the super jocks feel bad about themselves, because this is the age when no one likes themselves." This made Eric realize he was no different from others his age. Those words made him stop thinking about how he could take his life. His youth leaders surrounded him with the unconditional love of his heavenly Father, which was exactly what he needed more than anything else.

One day after youth group, his favorite leader sat down and talked to him about forgiveness. He said, "Jesus forgave you for all of your sins and took the punishment on Himself so you wouldn't have to go through that pain when you die. Now you have eternal life because of what Jesus did for you. All He asks in return, Eric, is that you forgive others like He forgave you. I'm telling you this because it is time you forgave your father for the hurt and pain that he has caused you and your family. If you don't forgive, the Bible says that you will not be forgiven either." Eric knew he needed forgiveness for the many thoughts, words, and deeds that he had committed in his fourteen years of life. He went on to say, "Forgiveness is a choice; it's not a feeling. Forgiveness is for your benefit more than for your father's. You see, when you refuse to forgive, a root of bitterness starts to grow in your soul. As it continues to grow, it squelches the happiness and peace that you once had. It chokes out the good stuff and leaves you miserable. I know that the hurt you are feeling is overwhelming to you, but forgiveness will start to bring healing and make you feel much better." Eric knew deep down inside of his spirit that what his counselor was saying was true. In fact, the burden of forgiveness he had been carrying around was weighing him down and making him miserable. He was no longer fun to be around and knew he needed to give up the heavy load he was trying to bear alone. That day Eric decided to forgive his father, as his youth pastor led him in a prayer of forgiveness. During the prayer, Eric felt the warm sensation of tears running down his face that he experienced at school, but these tears were different. They were tears of release and healing. As they closed in prayer, Eric felt a sense of weightlessness and was so grateful his youth leader had taken the time to share the truth with him. As soon as he made that decision to forgive, he felt like two big hands had pulled an enormous weight from his shoulders. He experienced a freedom he had never felt before, and peace flooded his body.

Eric not only became his former fun-loving self again, but he decided that he would spend time, after he graduated from school, mentoring teenagers, especially ones who were facing divorce in their families. He went to work with Project SOS as a fulltime mentor to teenagers in thirteen middle schools and high schools. He found his calling and started using the gifts God had given him, a compassionate heart and two listening ears. Today he's still an awesome role model for teens to follow. He's saving himself physically for his future wife and has avoided drugs and alcohol, because he learned how to have a great time without leaning on artificial substances to have fun. Eric knows very well that life has periodic bumps in the road, and with friends that truly care about his well being, he can overcome anything.

## Lessons learned:

1. We don't control other people's lives, and yes, life does hold some major hurts. After we have experienced pain, we become more compassionate and are more able to help others who are going through similar experiences.
2. Family is important. When one person leaves, the others need to cling together and become even stronger than they were before.
3. Divorce is painful. Married people need to make and keep a commitment to each other for life unless abuse is involved. Commitment means sticking together through the good and the bad and staying faithful to each other; otherwise someone will get hurt, usually the entire family.
4. Have mentors in your life. God brings others to you, especially when you are suffering. Lean on them. They are there to help you.
5. Forgiveness is a choice, not a feeling. It releases from bitterness the one who has forgiven, allowing them to live to the fullest.

## Scriptures to learn:

- …but there is a friend (Jesus) who sticks closer than a brother (Proverbs 18:24).

And we know that all things work together for good to those who love God, to those who are the called according to His purpose (Romans 8:28).
- Yet in all these things we are more than conquerors through Him who loved us (Romans 8:37).
- He who made them at the beginning made them male and female and said, 'For this reason a man shall leave

his father and mother and be joined to his wife, and the two shall become one flesh? So then, they are no longer two but one flesh. Therefore what God has joined together, let not man separate (Matthew 19:4-6).

- I say to you, whoever divorces his wife, except for sexual immorality, and marries another, commits adultery... (Matthew 19:9).

- Whenever you stand praying, if you have anything against anyone, forgive him, that your Father in heaven may also forgive you your trespasses. But if you do not forgive, neither will your Father in heaven forgive your trespasses (Mark 11:25-26).

# UNEXPECTED HERO

Born… at an inopportune time…

Shortly after birth… a violent death was to be his lot.

Moses' mother prayed… begging God to save her son.

By God's creative design…
Moses was saved… protected… and

Literally ushered into the Pharoah's household;

Into the house of the very man that wanted him dead.

Raised and schooled with
the best the world had to offer…

Given every advantage.

Then he learned of his heritage…
as a Jew… one of God's chosen people.

In his haste to help his people…
to be a hero… he killed a man…

and heaped trouble on the backs of his kinsmen…

So hated, misunderstood and judged by all….

He ran, a fugitive…
hiding on the backside of the desert…

Moses hid.

We are not told what he thought about…
just that he was a Shepherd…

caring for sheep.

Then… when Moses probably held no hope

For ever becoming anything more than a
Shepherd on the backside of the desert...

God called him... to the destiny he was BORN for:

To redeem God's chosen people...

and bring them out of captivity...

So too were YOU born for such a time as this...

with a destiny...to speak to YOUR generation...

A word of hope...from the LIVING GOD...

Be encouraged.... Listen...

And "GO TELL IT ON THE MOUNTAIN!

# SHE WAS ONLY AS SICK AS HER SECRETS

She was small for her age, but she made up for her tiny frame in her strong personality and big heart. She was quite daring, which brought her much attention in spite of her size. When Anne was fourteen, she had her first crush on a boy. He was seventeen and very handsome. She was enthralled with the fact that she could get a seventeen-year-old boyfriend, as young as she looked. When he called her on the phone, she thought her heart would pound out of her small-framed chest. They talked, shared notes, and she told him more than she had ever shared with anyone, even with her best friends. Then the day came when he asked her to meet him after school so they could go to his house. She knew her parents wouldn't find out because they were both at work. That morning, getting ready for school, she tried on what seemed to be every outfit in her closet before finding the one that would make her look at least sixteen. She grabbed her book bag and went off to the ivory towers of the very exclusive private school she was attending. Anne's grades were good, but she found it hard to concentrate during class that day. She had visions of her first boyfriend giving her the very first kiss she ever had. She imagined how sweet and tender that embrace would be. She was sure that he would tell her, "Anne, I love you more than I've ever loved anyone in my life." She couldn't wait for that dismissal bell to ring so she could go meet her "first love." She knew the exact spot to meet him so they could walk together hand-in-hand to his house.

When they arrived, they were alone. Both of his parents were at work, just like Anne's. He showed her around his beautiful house, then wasted no time before he took her to his bedroom. Once there, he pulled her down onto his bed and started kissing her. This was different than she had imagined. It was certainly not one bit tender nor was it very romantic. He never mentioned that he loved her, and after kissing her mouth and neck, he started taking off her top and unzipping her pants. That's when Anne started to push away and say, "Please stop this. I don't want to do this, so quit it!" He didn't stop. She started to panic and said the same "NO!" with more power in her voice, but he had a goal and, like a game hunter stalking his prey, Anne was being forced to submit to something she really had no intention of doing. When he had finished his act of date rape, Anne began to cry. He tried to pretend it was her fault for coming to his house looking so sexy and fine. All she wanted to do at that moment was to get away from this false Prince Charming.

Anne couldn't tell her parents what happened for fear that they would punish her for going to his home without his parents there, and not coming straight home from school as she should have done. So she decided to keep this horrible thing from them. The next day at school, Anne told her friends, hoping they would know what she should do and give her the sympathy and advice that she so desperately needed. Instead, they said, "Oh, well, you're not a virgin anymore. Join the club!" Anne was shocked that her closest friends would think so casually about something so traumatic that she had endured just the day before. Now, more than ever, she wanted to talk to her parents, but was too scared of what they would say. They would probably ground her, and she certainly didn't want to miss out on any fun. She wanted more freedom, not less, so she decided not to tell anyone else what had happened. She would just wear a mask and paste on a smile, all the while her heart was breaking underneath.

In front of her friends, she acted all tough like this rape didn't bother her, but deep down in her soul she needed someone who could tell her that the rape was not her fault. Instead, she learned very well how to put on her mask to cover her pain. That mask became her identity for the next several years.

Anne became a party girl with her friends. They would tell a few "white lies" to their parents about where they were going and end up at wild parties drinking, trying drugs, and having sex. This became the routine on weekends, until one day, Anne learned that she was pregnant. She was only fifteen, still making good grades, but totally confused as to how this could have happened to her instead of one of her friends. She tried to think back about the sex partners she'd had and if they had used protection each time, but her memory was blurred from the drugs and alcohol she took before going to bed with someone. In order to rationalize her predicament, she told herself that at least she didn't get an STD (sexually transmitted disease). She was only pregnant and that could be covered up with an abortion and her mask of cheer. She decided to do what the other good girls did at her school when they got pregnant. They took up a collection for Anne to go to Planned Parenthood to have an abortion. So on Saturday afternoon, her friends drove her to the abortion clinic to have the procedure done. She was shocked at the large number of teenagers in the waiting room. None were talking or looking at each other. All of them looked scared.

When the abortion was over, she felt hollow and empty inside. She knew she had just taken an innocent life and wondered if the other teens in the waiting room would feel similar emotions after their procedures. Again, she rationalized the situation away by saying, "What choice did I have?" As she walked slowly to the car where her friends were waiting, she put on her "mask of cover," acting like it was no big deal. When she got home, she went straight to her room and cried harder than she had ever cried before. Before long, her parents knocked on the door and entered to tell Anne some bad news: her favorite grandmother had just passed away. She thought for sure this was God's way of punishing her for taking the life of one of His creations. She became very angry with God and blamed Him for taking her grandmother. She became enraged whenever she heard the name of God or Jesus.

Anne started to sink deeper and deeper in her lifestyle of unhealthy choices. She really didn't care whether she lived or died, so she partied more and kept sleeping around. One thing that seemed to help was to write poetry about her feelings and her life. She would write about her unworthiness, her out-of-control life, and her dark secrets. She wanted, in the worst way, to talk to her parents, but she had so many secrets that she didn't even know where to start, so she never did. A voice in her mind would speak to her saying, "What would your parents think if their perfect little girl took off her mask and showed them who she really is? Don't you know that they would hate you and kick you out of the house?" That voice would torment her at night, especially in her dreams. That one voice would eventually become the voices of many, to the point where Anne thought she was going crazy and knew she had to talk to someone she could trust.

She had watched one particular teacher whom the students liked very much and talked to after class. One day, she mustered up the nerve to ask him if she could make an appointment to talk with him. He was so friendly and said, "Sure, but you don't need an appointment; just come here to my room after school today." She finally felt some relief, but she worried how much she should tell him the first time she talked to him. After their first visit, she felt somewhat better that someone else knew about her secret life, other than the demons that tormented her in the night.

This popular male teacher listened to Anne for several weeks, until he started to see Anne as a vulnerable young lady. One afternoon, after school, when they were alone in his classroom, he kissed her for the first time. It was a tender kiss like a first kiss should be, unlike her first kiss when she was 14 years old. Immediately, she started to have feelings for this teacher who was old enough to be her father. They started to see each other off campus at his place. There they could have sex and no one would know about it. At first she was caught up in a whirlwind of emotions. Sometimes she was excited to see her hero, and other days she was disgusted that he was still talking to other female students. She wondered if he was sleeping with them too. After some time had passed, she started to feel used and wondered how many other innocent victims he had lured into his web of deception.

Anne's mind was now the battlefield that she had to overcome every minute of every day. Somehow she was smart enough to maintain good grades so her parents stayed off her back, but their relationship was nonexistent. Sometimes in her bedroom, when she was all alone, Anne would take off her mask just long enough to see how miserable her life had become. She really only wanted to be a little girl again, but was caught up living an adult lifestyle that was more than cruel to her. To mask the pain, she would do more drugs and drink more heavily. Eventually, those temporary fixes stopped working. She was then faced with the reality of her poor choices and the feelings of guilt and shame that were overwhelming to her.

Finally, these feelings had become more than she knew how to handle, so she made a plan to take her life. Her father had beautiful hunting guns. Anne spent more than one night looking at those guns, contemplating suicide. Each time she was ready to do it, she would feel regret that her parents would find her body and have that memory haunting them for the rest of their lives. She knew about the pain of bad memories, and she didn't want them to suffer what she had suffered for the past several years.

One of the voices in her mind, that visited her regularly, suggested that she could starve herself to death and no one would know it was suicide. This way her parents would deal with the gradual death of their daughter, not a sudden, violent suicidal death. This would be much less painful for them and a whole lot less messy. As she stopped eating, she felt better, almost as though she was punishing herself for all of the unhealthy choices she had made.

Anne had gone from being an outgoing, confident preteen living a privileged lifestyle, to someone living under total deception leading to low self-esteem, hopelessness, and suicidal tendencies. She was on the slippery slope Hollywood never tells teenagers about as their movies glorify sex, drugs, and alcohol. Hollywood's form of fun had taken its toll on Anne, like millions of other vulnerable teenagers experience each year. She had learned the hard way that sex is more than a physical act. She now knew it was also emotional, psychological, social, and spiritual. She was finally able to discern Hollywood's mask as it parades itself around in the form of fun for the popular crowd, each actor wearing the same, identical mask that Anne had been wearing since she was fourteen. They were all in attendance looking beautiful on the outside while dying of pain on the inside. All had on their beautiful face paint like circus clowns pretending to be having fun. Together, they were at the greatest masquerade ball of all: life.

Anne found herself pregnant again at age seventeen. Once more she traveled down that all too familiar road to reenact the same procedure that would end yet another life. As before, her parents would be the last to know and depression would return to visit.

Anne had come to the conclusion that starvation wasn't all that bad. It gave her something to focus on instead of her regrets and overwhelming feelings of depression. She actually enjoyed running several miles every night, because the endorphins being released in her brain gave her some feeling of elation. This starvation game actually made her feel like she was back in control of her life, which was a feeling she hadn't experienced since she was fourteen. She could control her decision to refuse food, and she was so good at deception that she would take her dinner to her room so her parents thought she was eating while doing her homework. Her behaviors were truly becoming more and more bizarre. She would eat her dinner in her room, then throw up everything that was in her stomach into plastic containers and hide them under her bed before leaving the house to go jogging for several miles. Upon returning from her run she would shower, take several laxatives and go to sleep. Her laxative intake increased monthly and so did her inability to sleep. She would roll around on her bedroom floor in such great pain from stomach cramps, but was unable to stop the ritual to which she had become addicted. Food had now become Anne's total obsession.

Her parents noticed she was losing weight in her senior year, in spite of the baggy clothes she wore to try to hide her ever-decreasing frame. This eating disorder had conquered her mind, body and spirit.

When graduation finally arrived, Anne walked to the podium weighing thirty pounds less than normal. She was proud she had finished her swanky college prep school and was off to the University of Florida. She thought, "At last I'm away from family, so-called friends, and all of my past." She was so looking forward to total freedom, but what she didn't realize was that she was truly in bondage with no visible escape. Her addiction and the voices in her head would follow her wherever she tried to escape.

After her first semester of college, she returned home, suffering a total emotional and physical breakdown. Her parents had her admitted to an eating disorder clinic. Before leaving for the clinic, Anne decided to tell her parents everything. She didn't even care if they kicked her out of the house, because she felt numb most of the time anyway. The only thoughts she had were about her obsession with food. As she sat together with her parents, she decided to peel off her mask layer by layer. She had never done this before. As she took off the first layer the others started to peel more quickly while she poured out her heart and revealed her lifestyle. She began with what had happened to her at the age of fourteen. As she shared her secret life with the two people who had created her, both her mother and father started to cry. They heard how their little girl had gone though all of those adult situations alone. They felt an overwhelming burden because they were not able to help her. They knew parents were to share in the hard times as well as the good, and felt guilty that they had missed this. Were they unavailable, tuned out because of their business, or just not seeing Anne's need? Questions and doubts raced through their minds as they took part of the blame for what had happened. Both of them cried for the part that they had played in the drama of their daughter's shipwrecked life. That night the three of them stayed up for hours crying and talking. The next day Anne left for the clinic. Her parents were left feeling remorse, fear and disappointment over how things had turned out in their family.

After three months, the insurance company refused to pay any more of the expensive costs for Anne to receive treatment, so she returned home. She had received some help during that stay and had time to write lots of poems. Many were very dark, describing the enemy of her soul. He had come to her at first looking like a friend, almost like an angel of light, but turned on her in order to rob, kill, and destroy her mind, emotions, intellect and, of course, her body.

One morning, while drinking my coffee and reading the morning newspaper, I saw a picture of Anne in the paper and read the article about her eating disorder. As I looked at the pictures of Anne's tiny, bony body, great compassion came over me. After reading the article, I knew I was supposed to contact her to see if she wanted to speak publicly to teenagers in local schools. When she answered the phone, I could hear a bubbly, outgoing voice on the other end. I told her about my staff of young adults, all willing to share their stories with teens in order to help change the youth culture for the better. She said with great joy in her voice, "Yes, I would love to help other kids avoid what happened to me by sharing my testimony!" I knew I was going to have a divine meeting with her the next day at our office.

As she entered our office door, her smile lit up the entire room. I felt compelled to give her a hug. When I did, I felt like I was touching a baby bird that had fallen out of its nest before it had grown feathers. I could feel every bone in her small-framed body. As we sat down to talk in my office, I couldn't help but notice that her hands were nothing but bones and joints, covered by sagging skin. We sat and talked for over an hour.

I invited several of my young adult staff to share their testimonies with Anne. As she listened, she realized that other people had gone through major setbacks in their lives also, but were now overcoming them by sharing their testimonies with teens in order to help them avoid the pitfalls that they had fallen prey to. After the other staff members left the room, I held Anne's hand with her palm upturned and asked her if she understood why she was the only one with those exact fingerprints. She wasn't sure what I meant, so I shared with her that she was unique, one of a kind, created for a purpose that God had planned for her. She was so receptive that I felt led to share with her about the free gift of salvation. She really was interested in the part about receiving forgiveness from every thing she had ever done because of Jesus' willingness to pay the penalty for those sins. As I started to share the gospel, she interrupted me and said, "I want that for myself. Whatever it is that all of you have, please let me have it!" I felt so very privileged to be able to pray for Anne to ask Christ into her heart, to let Him take the reins of her life and use it for His purposes. After we prayed she said something I will never forget: "I have been fighting against religion most of my life, and now I'm receiving what I hated so much." I corrected her gently by saying, "You've not been given religion. You now have started a personal relationship with your Creator who loves you more than you'll ever be able to fathom. You're going to be healed, set free, and delivered from all that has been controlling and tormenting you since you were fourteen. You will never be the same again." We both cried and hugged before she left this divine appointment that God had supernaturally arranged for us. She agreed to come see a program the very next day so she could see how we changed the hearts of teenagers.

The next morning, she came to the office at 6:00 a.m.. I was there early, as well, so we were able to spend some time together before leaving to see the program. She watched the program intently while learning about STDs and other facts about drugs and alcohol she had not been exposed to at her private school. She laughed at our funny skits and cried during the powerful testimonies. At the end of the two-hour health program, this little sixty pound anorexic young lady was so exhausted that she slept all the way back to the office.

For the next six months Anne spoke to thousands of middle school and high school students. During the first month, while standing in front of one of her high school audiences, she started to cry and said she couldn't do it. Most of the young adult Project SOS speakers go through this stage of healing when they first start to share the pain in their lives. The more they speak, and as more healing takes place, the less they cry, until they are able to work through the pain and become victors over their past experiences. Eventually the painful memories become just distant remembrances used to help others avoid making the same mistakes.

When I saw her crying, I walked forward, put my arm around her, and gave her testimony myself to the classroom full of students while she stood next to me, with her head on my shoulder, crying. When I had finished, she found the courage to read one of her poems and talk to them about the importance of communicating to their parents when things go wrong. That same group of teenagers gave her a standing ovation and wrote her many notes and letters of encouragement. Girls wrote about having eating disorders, and how they had decided to go home to talk to their moms about their problems. Others, who had experienced abortions, could identify with her feelings of emptiness. They also agreed to go tell their parents so their healing could begin. It was obvious that very day that Anne was destined for greatness and was starting to fulfill her God-given destiny.

Six months later, Anne was admitted to a free research hospital for eating disorders where she gained over fifty pounds. She went on to work in the food industry in New York City. She proved to herself that she was more capable than ever before and is living a successful, independent life today.

**Lessons learned:**

1. No matter what has happened to you, whether it was your fault or not, it is important to tell at least one of your parents.
2. I have taught hundreds of thousands of teenagers that all thought that their parents would kill them if they told them what was truly going on in their lives. By the way, none who told are dead.
3. I've attended numerous funerals of teenagers who have died because of sex, drugs, alcohol, and suicide. Most of their parents were not told about the magnitude of the problems their teenager was experiencing until after the funeral.
4. Many families are closer than ever because their children started to confide in them. You see, parents do love their children more than anyone else in the world. They may be disappointed when teens tell them some truths, but they will always love them.
5. Base your self-image on what God's Word (the Bible) says about you, not on what the advertising and media industry tells you. You'll never be able to live up to their standards, so quit trying! Did you know that their job is to make you unhappy with the way you are so you'll feel compelled to buy something they're selling?
6. Reach out today to someone who needs you. True contentment comes from giving time, treasure, or talent to someone else in need.

**Scriptures to learn:**

- (Jesus is talking about people who hurt children): But whoever causes one of these little ones who believe in Me to stumble, it would be better for him if a millstone were hung around his neck, and he were thrown into the sea (Mark 9:42).

- For we must all appear before the judgment seat of Christ, that each one may receive the things done in the body, according to what he has done, whether good or bad (2 Corinthians 5:10).
- For nothing is secret that will not be revealed, nor anything hidden that will not be known and come to light (Luke 8:17).
- He has made everything beautiful in its time. He has put eternity in their hearts (Eccles. 3:11).
- For Satan himself transforms himself into an angel of light (2 Corinthians 11:14).
- Finally, my brethren, be strong in the Lord and in the power of His might. Put on the whole armor of God, that you may be able to stand against the wiles of the devil. For we do not wrestle against flesh and blood, but against principalities, against powers, against the rulers of the darkness of this age, against spiritual hosts of wickedness in the heavenly places. Therefore take up the whole armor of God, that you may be able to withstand in the evil day, and having done all, to stand. Stand therefore, having girded your waist with truth, having put on the breastplate of righteousness, and having shod your feet with the preparation of the gospel of peace; above all, taking the shield of faith with which you will be able to quench all the fiery darts of the wicked one. And take the helmet of salvation, and the sword of the Spirit, which is the word of God; praying always with all prayer and supplication in the Spirit, being watchful to this end with all perseverance and supplication for all the saints (Ephesians 6:10-18).

- The thief *(the devil)* does not come except to steal, and to kill, and to destroy. I *(Jesus)* have come that they may have life, and that they may have it more abundantly (John 10:10).

# JESUS KNEW

Jesus knew He was the fulfillment of
those who had gone before.

Jesus knew He was a warrior in a real and vicious war.

Jesus knew His enemy was real, and that he came to kill.

Jesus knew the mission that He came to fulfill.

By far the most important thing that Jesus knew,

Is the honest complete picture of the truth of me and you.

He knew each intricate detail…
every sin, every mistake…

Those things never made Him question the road
He chose to take.

So when the enemy comes in accusing
you for all the things you do,

Put your trust in God alone… and always know

that Jesus knew…

Katherine Denham Osgood

# TRUE LOVE

Crystal and Jacob met in middle school. She thought he was cute, and the fact that he played football really didn't hurt, either. He thought she was adorable. She was the shortest girl in his school with the biggest blue eyes he had ever seen. Officially they didn't start going out until their last year in middle school. "Going out" meant talking on the phone, seeing each other during youth group at their local church, and holding hands while walking down the hallways at school. They were "an item" and everyone knew them as the cutest couple on the middle-school campus. Then, when they graduated from junior high, they had to say good-bye in a sense, because they were going to attend separate high schools. They planned to see each other on the weekends, at his football games and her soccer games, and at youth group on Wednesday and Sunday evenings. They would also talk on the phone every night, sharing their dreams and goals and talking about how much they cared for each other.

Jacob found out about Project SOS from his football buddies. He had a group of guys who held each other accountable. They made an agreement that all of them would wait for sex until marriage and none would start drinking or doing drugs like many of their other team-mates. They would also recruit others to join them, regardless of their past choices. They would hang out together with their dates on the weekends, on "away" football trips, during summer camp, and see each other at their youth groups. They all decided they would volunteer for Project SOS so they could help the middle school students avoid making some of the mistakes their class-mates were making.

These big jocks, after being dismissed from class and still wearing their football jerseys, would drive over to a middle school, present a Project SOS program, and talk to the teens about making and keeping a commitment to abstinence from sex, drugs, and alcohol. They would give their personal testimonies about how they held each other accountable. Jacob would bring a picture of Crystal and talk about how much he loved her. The girls in the audi-ence would make appreciative sounds of approval but the boys, being too cool, would not dare say a word, but they listened to everything Jacob said. Then Jacob would share that he and Crystal had agreed to a physical boundary of not going past kissing until their wedding night, if and when they would get married. He also shared that they never went into each other's homes when parents were away. If they happened to arrive before their parents, they would sit on the front steps or in the driveway talking. He told the teens to go out in groups and stay in public places where other people could see and hear them in case they needed help. Jacob would tell the girls, "If a guy doesn't respect you and your commitment to abstinence, dump him! He is not worth your time. You are too valuable to be used by some guy who doesn't care what happens to you."

The girls would applaud Jacob and his ability to see their hearts and know what they wanted and needed to hear. All the girls had dreams of meeting their very own Jacob. He was very muscular and strong and very courageous to speak with such authority. They idolized him and thought Crystal must be one of the luckiest girls in the world.

After seeing the STD power-point presentation, skits, demonstrations, and testimonies, the football players would encourage the teens to sign the commitment card that was in their health packet supplied by Project SOS. Almost all of the teens did. After answering questions from the audience, the players would ask the eighth graders, "How many of you are coming to our game Friday night?" Most of the audience of 300 teenagers would raise their hands. Then they would say, "Look for our numbers on the field and know that we are the strongest ones out there, not only physically, but morally and emotionally. Take our lead, get an accountability group, make a pact to live life to the fullest without sex, drugs, and alcohol, and know that you can do it! We are proud of you and believe in you!" The students would not only applaud them but would ask for their autographs. They were the local heroes every school needed. They had the guts to speak up and make a difference in their youth culture. They knew they could make a difference and took the time to encourage younger students to live a life of moral integrity and health. None of them had any regrets. None of them stayed up awake at night wondering if they had gotten a girl pregnant. None of them had to visit the local health department to get tested for STDs; none of them had to live with the fear that an STD would cause them to become sterile or contract genital cancers. None of them had to take a girlfriend to get a pregnancy test.

None of them cared what other guys thought about them or said to them, because they were the strong ones and they knew it. They could resist negative peer pressure because they were brave, true leaders who had each other to lean on when times got tough and temptation was knocking at the door of their hearts, minds, and bodies. They had more fun than any of the other teammates because they made a choice for ultimate freedom from worry, regret, fear, shattered dreams, and goals. They had self-respect, boundaries, confidence and the admiration of all who knew them.

While still in high school, Jacob and Crystal volunteered as a couple during weekend programs. They were so cute and all of the students admired their commitment, their boundaries, and their love for each other. I hoped and prayed I would be able to have the funding to hire them as paid presenters when they graduated.

God was faithful. The Monday after their high school graduation they came to work for Project SOS as program presenters during the day and attended college in the evenings. They were such an outstanding couple. They performed skits, did demonstrations, and gave the most romantic testimony about their relationship. Jacob would challenge the audience to a dance contest and students had so much fun competing with him. Laughter is one way of reaching teenagers, and Jacob truly knew how to make them laugh. Crystal was much more reserved than Jacob. In fact, the first time she stepped on stage to speak, she burst into tears. After realizing that I was not going to let her quit, she became a very outstanding speaker. Most of all, the students in middle schools and high schools loved seeing a couple who was madly in love but choosing to wait until marriage before sharing the greatest gift they had: their virginity. They had seen so much Hollywood sex in movies and TV that they had no idea what true romance looked like, and the teens loved learning what a truly healthy relationship looked like.

After being program presenters, Crystal and Jacob became full time mentors for all of the middle schools in three counties. They would travel hours each day getting to their schools, setting up the clubs, and encouraging the teens in attendance by helping them learn the skills necessary to keep a commitment from all unhealthy relationships. In addition to their mentoring, they were being invited to do radio interviews and were featured in stories in local and state papers and magazines. They were getting the attention that most teenagers were seeking because of the decisions they had made to live a life free from unhealthy choices.

One day Crystal walked into our office wearing a beautiful engagement ring. Actually, the entire staff knew when and how Jacob was going to propose to her before it happened. He planned a fun evening with their friends. First, he took her to dinner on a balcony that overlooked the bay and the Bridge of Lions in the oldest city in the nation, St. Augustine, Florida. After they finished a romantic dinner, he got down on one knee and proposed to her. After she received her ring, Jacob had arranged for all their friends to meet them in a stretch limo. It was such a romantic evening! To top it off, they made a commitment to stop kissing during their engagement and wait for ten months to seal their wedding with a kiss at the alter when the minister said, "You may now kiss the bride!"

Ten months later, Jacob and Crystal did walk down the aisle to be married. It was the most beautiful wedding because of their beautiful relationship. They did wait through their entire engagement for that special kiss at the end of the aisle. They both said it was worth the wait. The reception was beautiful, the decorations magnificent, and the food delicious. It was a perfect evening for the perfect couple.

Prior to their wedding they attended pre-marital classes at their church and read a book about how to give your total body to your mate on your wedding night. During the reception, Jacob teased Crystal saying, "Can we leave yet?" That night they consummated their love for each other with no regrets about waiting, bonding together for life and carrying no negative baggage into their marriage. They became one in flesh as they gave their entire body, mind, and soul to each other that special night. They had never even liked someone else or held another person's hand in a romantic way. They shared their first kiss ever and their first intimate moment. Neither one had ever shared that special gift with anyone else. **Now <u>that's</u> true love.**

### Lessons Learned:

1. God tells us to wait because He wants the best for His children. He wants your wedding to be one of a kind. He wants your honeymoon to be the most romantic evening of your life. He wants you to have total freedom to love your mate until death separates you . He wants the best sex for you, and that is found in a faithful, committed marriage. Don't settle for an imitation. Hold out for the best. You deserve it.
2. Good things come to those who wait. Jacob and Crystal became known throughout the entire area because of their commitment. They were featured in a state magazine, on the radio, and on television. Fame for doing the right thing is, oh, so sweet!

3. To keep a commitment to abstinence from sex, drugs, and alcohol you will need to set four types of boundaries.

   <u>Physical boundaries:</u> Know where you will stop and don't go past that point. Keep your clothes on. Crystal and Jacob stopped at kissing so neither one of them would get "turned on" before their wedding night. They didn't make out and touch each other's body parts. If you do kiss, stand up or sit down; avoid lying down. Explain your boundaries before going out with someone. If that person doesn't respect your boundaries, don't waste your time. You deserve better and must expect respect.

   <u>People boundaries:</u> Only date people with the same commitment. Don't assume anyone has made a commitment; ask. Find accountability partners like Jacob and Crystal had. Find friends that will help you be a better person. Unhealthy friends will always drag you down. You won't be able to pull them up.

   <u>Place boundaries:</u> Stay out of empty houses. Go in groups and stay in public places. If drugs and alcohol are being used at a party, leave. Make your own party. It will be more fun with no regrets in the morning.

   <u>Time boundaries:</u> The longer the time you spend alone with someone you are attracted to, the harder it is to avoid temptation. Avoid late night conversations on the phone because you'll be more tempted to talk about sex.

## Scriptures to learn:

- But now I have written to you not to keep company with anyone named a brother, who is sexually immoral, or covetous, or an idolater, or a reviler, or a drunkard, or an extortioner—not even to eat with such a person (1 Corinthians 5:11).

- Eye has not seen, nor ear heard, nor have entered into the heart of man the things which God has prepared for those who love Him (1 Corinthians 2:9).
- Do not be unequally yoked together with unbelievers. For what fellowship has righteousness with lawlessness? And what communion has light with darkness (2Corinthians 6:14)?
- For do I now persuade men, or God? Or do I seek to please men? For if I still pleased men, I would not be a bondservant of Christ (Galatians 1:10).
- Walk in the Spirit, and you shall not fulfill the lust of the flesh. For the flesh lusts against the Spirit, and the Spirit against the flesh... (Galatians 5:16-17).
- Flee also youthful lusts; but pursue righteousness, faith, love, peace with those who call on the Lord out of a pure heart (2 Timothy 2:22).
- For this is the will of God, your sanctification: that you should abstain from sexual immorality, that each of you should know how to possess his own vessel in sanctification and honor, not in passion of lust... (1 Thessalonians 4:3-5).
- Therefore a man shall leave his father and mother and be joined to his wife, and they shall become one flesh. And they were both naked, and the man and his wife, and were not ashamed (Genesis 2:24-25).

# Two Made One

Two made one…
A very sacred union of two special chosen vessels:
United in His love.
But look back down the journey's road with me for a
while,
And see the Father's handiwork; observe His gentle style.
As He takes each heart and makes it truly His,
In the midst of yielded wholeness, that is where His
blessing is.
In the midst of yielded wholeness, where our hearts are
in full view,
And through the Father's awesome grace He is made
Lord of you.
An often very painful process… not for the weak of
heart….
That is where true unity finds its enduring
start…
From there you grow in love preferring first the
other,
Learning how to walk in grace beside our
brother…
Two becoming one, a blessing we cannot
anticipate…
Yes, my friend… the prize truly goes to those who
wait….

Katherine Denham Osgood

# SUICIDE:
# NO LONGER AN OPTION

Mark had always felt different for as long as he could remember. He didn't fit into the regular scene. He didn't like sports, preppy clothes, or traditional music. He liked punk rock and heavy metal music; he liked body piercing, weird clothing, drama, and wild hair colors and styles.

When Mark showed up at my office for an interview, he and his two friends were three hours late, having driven to another state before noticing they had passed their exit! Mark was wearing an orange shirt with some kind of design all over it, a pair of tight black jeans, pink high top tennis shoes and a metal belt injected with silver bullets. He had pierced eyebrows and ears and would soon have his lip pierced. Oh, did I mention that his hair was half purple and half bright yellow? I hired him on the spot after sensing his enthusiasm for wanting to help teenagers. He was shocked. He said to me, "I can't believe I have found a person that will not only hire me, but wants me to look weird! Most interviewers said I would have to change my entire look if I wanted to work for them, that's if they even wanted to interview me after looking at me!"

I needed his looks in order to reach a very special group of punk rockers and gothic teens that would not receive the message of abstinence from a jock or preppy. As Mark got up to leave the interview, I made him promise not to change his looks unless he was going to look even wilder, and then he had my permission to do so. He gave me a big hug, told me how much he appreciated the opportunity to change the youth culture for the better, and off he went with his two buddies. Hopefully they found their way back home without ending up in another state again!

Mark had just graduated from high school where he was well known for his appearance and drama skills. He was also a musician in a Christian, punk-rock band. He played bass guitar and wrote music. He had a heart as big as Texas and a smile that would light up any room. He was extremely funny and soft spoken, but when he did speak, everyone listened.

Mark had no concept of time, which should have been obvious to me after his tardiness for his interview. He had a very hard time going to bed before 1:00 or 2:00 a.m., even when he knew he'd have to get up at 4:30 a.m to drive one hour to our office, to then prepare to leave by 6:00 a.m. for a school program. One day he wanted to surprise us, so he got to the office early. He was so proud of himself. Instead of going to bed that night, he just decided to stay up all night so he wouldn't be late for work! When he drove into the company parking lot, seeing no other cars there, he parked, turned off the ignition, put his seat in the recline position and got some badly needed shut-eye. The only problem was that no one knew he was there. The team waited for an extra 30 minutes, which was not unusual for us to do for Mark. We finally gave up on waiting for him and drove off, not knowing we were leaving him in the parking lot sound asleep. In fact, he was still asleep in the same spot when our team returned from our school program at 4:00 in the afternoon! The commotion of our team as they climbed out of the company van talking, laughing, and cutting up is what woke him up! Mark eventually became much better at punctuality as the months rolled by and his wallet became lighter. He needed money to pay for his apartment, car insurance, and gas. Growing up took some time, but the option of moving back home was the inspiration that motivated him to get to bed earlier and have his accountability partner call him every morning to see that he was awake.

When Mark got up in front of an audience of middle school or high school students, there would always be some wisecracks made. Usually the laughter and snide remarks were coming from the table filled with the jocks. But as soon as he started to speak, everyone listened, even the jocks.

He would start by telling a story about his best friend named Pam. Right after high school graduation, she found out that she was pregnant. Not being married or having a boyfriend, and being a recreational drug user who didn't have a steady job, Pam was convinced that she only had one option: abortion. She went to the abortion clinic after borrowing $450 dollars, had her abortion, left the clinic and went right back to her part-time job of building fences on a golf course.

Three months later, Pam became very ill. The company she was working for had hired her full-time which meant she had benefits. When they found out how sick she was, they sent her to the emergency room. When the doctor came in, she told him that her back was killing her and she was having trouble urinating. She also had a very high fever. They wanted to do an X-ray, but wanted to make sure she wasn't pregnant before doing so. When they asked if she could be pregnant, she sheepishly told them, "No, I had an abortion three months ago and haven't had sex since that time." They insisted on her taking a pregnancy test so the hospital would not be liable, if by any stretch of the imagination, she could have been pregnant. She reluctantly took the test, knowing there was no way it would turn out positive.

The doctor came into the room, closed the curtain behind him, and told Pam, "You have a very severe kidney infection and you are still pregnant, Pam. The abortion did not work." She was totally in shock! What did this mean? What should she do now? Would she have to miss days from work? Would they fire her? Feeling totally overwhelmed, she started to cry. Slowly, she looked up at the doctor and with tears running down her cheeks asked, "What should I do? I'm so scared." The doctor said, "Pam, this is a decision you will have to make on your own. All I can tell you is if you carry the baby it could be missing arms or legs or both. In fact, the baby could have severe brain damage from the procedure they used to abort the fetus." Pam, still weeping, asked for a few minutes alone so she could make the most important decision she had ever had to make in her nineteen years of living: what to do about the baby she was still carrying.

Pam was not a religious person. In fact, she had never really prayed before, didn't much think it would help, but at this very moment for the first time she said, "God, if you are there, help me know what to do." Tears continued to flow down her cheeks onto the hospital gown.

When the doctor returned after several minutes, she had made up her mind. She would carry the baby to full term. Even in the midst of all the fear that was over-whelming her, the decision to not abort the baby again gave her great peace and comfort.

Four months later a baby boy was born to Pam. He was two months premature and only weighed two pounds. He was so small that he could fit in the palm of her hand. He had both arms and legs and was not damaged by the suction during the abortion. He spent the next two months in the hospital until he was healthy enough to be brought home.

Mark then tells his audience, "Pam is not only my best friend, but she's my mother, as well. I am that tiny baby that was born prematurely. I'm six feet tall and have both arms and legs, but sometimes I wonder if I'm brain damaged or not!" His audience would gasp at what he had just said, but then they would start to laugh about the brain-damaged part. He would continue, "My mother never told me the story about my life until I turned eigh-teen years old. She didn't want to share that kind of thing with a child. When she told me just a couple of months ago, I cried. All of my life I had hated myself. Many nights I would spend thinking about how I could kill myself and make it look like an accident. Then I found out that I could have been killed instead of being born! My mother cried when I told her about my suicidal thoughts and plans. We hugged and cried together for some time."

Mark would always add, "I share this true story about my life with you, because you too could have been aborted. Your mother didn't have to keep you. We are all very valuable and I know that I have a purpose for my life and so do you. That's why I am here to tell you that you matter. Since my mother told me about my birth, I no longer think about suicide. My life was spared so I could be here today to tell you that your life matters. If you are thinking about suicide or feel depressed, talk to a trusted adult today so you can get help."

Mark would finish his testimony with this: "By the way, contrary to what most of you might think, I have never done drugs, gotten drunk, or had sex. I do value my health, even though I like to look weird." Each time Mark ended his story and our program concluded, students would stay after to tell him how much they'd needed to hear what he said about valuing their lives. Thousands of lives have been changed by his message, and suicide is no longer an option for them, because Mark fulfilled the destiny God had for his life.

## Lessons learned:

1. Every life has value, including yours.
2. Suicide is a permanent decision to a temporary problem.
3. Never judge a book by the cover. Look at the heart of a person, not their appearance, to know what their character is like.
4. Diversity is good. It makes life interesting. If we all looked alike, how boring would that be?
5. Don't stereotype people by how they dress or look. Mark looked like a drug user, yet never got involved in unhealthy choices in his life.

## Scriptures to learn:

• Your eyes saw my substance, being yet unformed. And in Your book they were all written, the days fashioned for me, when as yet there were none of them (Psalm 139:16:).

- Trust in the Lord with all your heart, and lean not on your own understanding; in all your ways acknowledge Him, and he shall direct your path (Proverbs 3:5-6).
- He has strengthened the bars of your gates; He has blessed your children within you (Psalm 17:13).
- For I know the thoughts that I think toward you, says the Lord, thoughts of peace and not of evil, to give you a future and a hope. Then you will call upon Me and go and pray to Me, and I will listen to you . (Jeremiah 29:11-12).

Pam helps run a crisis pregnancy center. Like her son, she is also fulfilling her destiny to change the youth culture for the better.

# A MILLION TO ONE

A million to one…

Those are the odds that the you,
that is you, would be born….

You've seen it or heard how many
sperm fight for the right to

Fertilize the egg that becomes you…

A million to one…

Those are the odds of the existence of you

Specifically you…

Regress with me a moment to consider that
God spoke all creation into being!!!

He **spoke** and the moon and the stars were…

He **spoke** and the waters filled the earth…

He **spoke** and fish filled the sea…

Then… when it was time to create man…

He **formed** us with His hands… in His image…

Then gave us **HIS** breath of life;

You were formed by the very hand of
God in your mother's womb…

planned for by the Sovereign King of all creation…

then… if that were not enough …
He breathed His life into you!!!

You are here because He created you…

The ultimate Creator, Himself, created you…

Specifically… uniquely to show forth

His nature… His love … His mercy…

In a very special way… that only YOU can.

Now go forth… stand tall and strong…
run with the vision…

(don't be scared if it is unique)

That He has given you….

YOU MATTER!!!...to God!!!


Katherine Denham Osgood

# OVERCOMING ALL OF THE ODDS

Beating the odds was Marc's way of life. From the time he was a toddler growing up in a housing project, Marc has overcome all of the odds concerning how his life was supposed to have happened. He was born to a mother addicted to crack. She couldn't care for Marc because of her addiction, so he tried to raise himself. He would get up in the mornings, go to the kitchen, and open the refrigerator. The usual two things were in there: mayonnaise and bread. He would keep a knife near the floor so he could make his own sandwiches. After all, he was too small to reach the counter tops. He always ate the same two things, mayonnaise and bread. Marc didn't know that other people had something different for breakfast, lunch, and dinner. He was used to making his own mayo sandwiches whenever he was hungry. He thought that everyone ate like he did and dressed by themselves and got to the pre-school bus on time. This was normal life for Marc, because he had never known anything different.

Marc had no supervision. He was allowed to walk the streets at night and remembers being picked up by the police and brought home when he was around four years old. He didn't think he was doing anything wrong, just walking down the street after midnight. There was nothing unusual about that for him. He thought that everyone did that.

When Marc was five, several people from the state of Georgia came to his apartment and told him that he was going to live in a foster home so he would be in a better environment.

There were lots of other children at the foster home. Marc recalls one incident when his foster mother thought that the birthmark on his arm was dirt, so she filled a bathtub up with bleach and hot water and put him into it. She scrubbed his arm over and over again, but the marks never disappeared and neither did that painful childhood memory ever leave the recesses of his mind and emotions.

After several years of court battles, Marc's father finally got custody of him. He was now allowed to leave foster care and live with the person he needed the most, his dad. Soon after his arrival, his stepmother and dad noticed that his breathing was very raspy and shallow. When they took him to the doctor, Marc was immediately sent to a heart specialist, then a lung specialist. The diagnosis was serious as well as potentially fatal. Marc was born with his heart turned around backwards and on the right side of his body in his chest cavity and blood vessels wrapped around his lungs. His throat was closed almost completely shut, forcing him to take short and raspy breaths. The doctors told his parents that he probably wouldn't live past the age of ten, because as his body grew larger, the enlarged blood vessels would grow also, cutting off his windpipe and crushing his lungs. Against all odds, Marc has now reached his 21$^{st}$ birthday and stands over six feet tall. He is now able to breathe better than ever.

Marc joined Project SOS when he was almost twenty years old. He wanted to rap his testimony so the teens could relate to his style of music. Marc had long dreadlocks, broad shoulders, and was a very handsome young man, dark-skinned and part African–American, part American Indian. In one of his raps, he encouraged his audiences to overcome their adversities and to set goals and never quit. In another he rapped about his life and one of the biggest mistakes he'd made: having sex before marriage. He thought having sex would help the relationship he had with his girlfriend, but instead sex destroyed it. Sex had become the focus of the relationship. The relationship they had known, which had been one built on communication, respect, and trust, started to dissolve. Eventually they broke up, and now Marc's heart was not only backwards, but broken as well. At the age of eighteen, with a broken heart and lots of regrets, he made a commitment to save himself for marriage.

During that time in Marc's life, feelings of depression came over his mind and body. He had many thoughts of suicide because of the sexual relationship that had ended. He couldn't shake the feelings of depression until one day a friend of his from work invited him to go to church with him. After visiting several times, Marc decided to join the church and even went on a mission trip with the youth group. He found unconditional love through the Christians he met.

He was praying one day about finding another job that would give him some satisfaction. That very day, another friend, who was working with Project SOS, asked him to apply to work at the company. He interviewed and within a month, started working in a field that not only brought great satisfaction, but also helped him set goals for his life and become totally healed from his childhood wounds.

Now, Marc doesn't have time for drugs, alcohol, or sex. He's too busy fulfilling his destiny. He's a role model and example for all teenagers, especially those living in housing projects or with a parent addicted to drugs, or a teen dealing with depression.

About a year ago he told me privately that he wanted to talk to his mother. He hadn't seen or heard from her since he was taken away at the age of five. I told Marc that with God all things are possible. We prayed and stood on the scripture that says, "Ask anything in my name and you will receive it." Within one week of the time we prayed he got the call. The school presenters were having lunch after a school presentation when Marc's cell phone rang. He looked at the number and didn't recognize it and was about to turn it off and ignore the call. Then something inside of him said, "Answer your phone." After he said, "Hello," he punched my arm and with a big smile mouthed the words, "It's her!" Not knowing whom he meant, I teased him by saying to the table of staff members, "He must have a new girlfriend that we don't know about!" We laughed, but his arm nudged me again to get my attention and he mouthed the words, "It's my mom!"

When they got off the phone, we started screaming and hugging and carrying on so loudly that I thought we would be asked to leave the restaurant. God is so faithful to His children! Marc and his mom made arrangements to meet and talk the very next week in Georgia. They spent an entire day together, talking, crying, and getting to know one another. His mother is now off drugs and is successfully raising other children that are Marc's new brothers and sisters. In addition, his dad and stepmother have been foster parents for several years, sometimes parenting five children at a time. Marc gets up early in the morning to help them get ready for school, stays up late at night helping them with their homework, and is like a big brother role-model to all of them. Some day Marc will be an awesome father and husband. Until then he is a hero to all of the foster kids he has helped raise and all the teens he has talked to since working for Project SOS. Marc is not only a conqueror; he's my hero.

## Lessons learned:

1. No matter how bad your circumstances might be, you can be a conqueror.
2. Share what you have been through with others so they can be encouraged and have hope.
3. What many children sometimes think is normal may not be normal at all, but a type of abuse.
4. Prayer really does work! God cares about every detail of our lives.
5. Sex becomes the focus of a relationship when it is practiced outside of marriage. Communication, respect, and trust usually decline after sex is introduced into a premarital relationship.
6. God is in charge of our health and can astound the doctors. He is still a miracle worker today!

## Scriptures to learn:

- Yet in all these things we are more than conquerors through Him who loved us (Romans 8:37).

- …with God all things are possible (Matthew 19:26).
- If you abide in me, and My words abide in you, you will ask what you desire, and it shall be done for you (John: 15:7).
- …and by His stripes we are healed (Isaiah 53:5). Stripes are the lashes Jesus took on His back from being whipped.
- Beloved, I pray that you may prosper in all things and be in heath, just as your soul prospers (3 John 1:2).
- And the Lord will make you the head and not the tail; You shall be above only, and not be beneath… (Deut 28:13).
- Do not be conformed to this world, but be transformed by the renewing of your mind, that you may prove what is that good and acceptable and perfect will of God (Romans 12:2).
- In every thing give thanks; for this is the will of God in Christ Jesus for you (1 Thessalonians 5:18).
- For we are His workmanship, created in Christ Jesus for good works, which God prepared beforehand that we should walk in them (Ephesians 2:10).

# VARIABLES

As a researcher, variables need to
be controlled, calculated and assigned.

The variables in life are a different thing...

Often we are blind to the variables
that are just around the bend;

And we are blind to our enemy who would like

All our hope to end.

In research, variables are planned,
and each scenario worked out...

It's not that neat and clean in life;

In fact, as God's child it's all about
trusting God with all the variables...

Things I could never see;

To hearken only to the Father's voice as He fashions me

In His image to be a vessel of
hope literally to the nations...

of His faithfulness and of His love.

We cannot control life's variables; do not be deceived,

but know eternal treasure will
abound to those who will believe...

Katherine Denham Osgood

# HE COULDN'T
# TRUST HIS NEIGHBORS

John's father worked and traveled a lot and was an avid sports fan. When he was at home, he and John watched sports on television together. It didn't matter what team was playing; they just wanted to watch sports. John knew he would be an athlete someday, starting with tee ball at the age of four.

When John was only seven years of age, his mother deserted the family. His older sister, who was a preteen, tried to be his mom, but was not capable of filling such a big responsibility. John, like all children that go through some kind of trauma, figured it must have been his fault. He thought he had to have done or said something wrong to cause her to leave. Feelings of abandonment, confusion and guilt flooded his young mind and emotions.

He was looking for someone to take care of him. John's father was out of town most of the week and his sister did the best she could, but she wasn't able to nurture him like a real mother could. Instead of going home to an empty house when he got off the school bus, he would go next door to his neighbor's house. The couple was really nice to John and fed him snacks whenever he arrived at their home. John felt secure and his emotions were starting to heal from his mother's departure. One afternoon, the neighbors told John they wanted to play a fun game with him. He went along with the game because he trusted them, but soon didn't feel comfortable playing. It wasn't a sport like John and his dad played on the weekends. It was different. John felt like this game was bad. He felt like he must be bad, too, for playing their game. When John got off the school bus each day, his neighbors would invite him over to their house. John wanted to be with someone and talk about his day, have a snack and have someone to look up to, but he didn't like playing this secret game. He didn't feel safe when they played with him. John didn't want to play anymore and told them so. They tried to convince him that it was fun and that he wasn't going to get hurt. John knew they were lying, because he already had been hurt.

One day, instead of getting off the bus near his house, John got off at an earlier bus stop that was near the park. He had brought his baseball mitt and a brand new ball to school. He had planned in the morning not to go home, but to visit the park that day instead. John met up with some older guys who included him in their game when they saw the brand new ball he had brought. He had a great afternoon, doing what he loved most.

As the sun started to set and it began to get dark, the guys all went home to their homecooked meals, but not John. He waited until it was dark before sneaking home to his house so his neighbors wouldn't see him. Once inside his own home, he locked the door, grabbed a snack, said "hi" to his sister and went up to his room to play and watch TV. He felt relief that he had pulled it off, a feeling he hadn't experienced for quite some time.

Day after day, John would hang out at the park until dark playing basketball or baseball, then sneak home in order to avoid his neighbors. John never told anyone about the game his neighbors made him play. He was too ashamed and he was scared of what they would do if he told. After all, they'd said it was a secret game that no one else could ever find out about.

As John grew up in age and size, he was always put on older teams for sports because he was such an outstanding athlete. At one point, when he was just a seventh grader, he was playing with high school seniors on a league team. When John finally entered high school, the baseball coach already knew him and knew he was a winner.

During John's junior year his dad took a job out of state. John told his dad that he needed to stay at his high school in order to get a scholarship to college. By this time John was the lead pitcher on his team, pitching over ninety miles per hour. Scouts were coming from across the nation to watch him pitch. His dad agreed that it was best for John to stay at the same school, so he put him up in his own apartment and paid all the bills.

What do you think a star athlete at sixteen years of age and with his own apartment was up to? You guessed it: no good. John's place became the party place every night except the night before a ball game. John never studied, but his coaches covered for him and got his teachers to pass him so he could play ball. John had become very experienced in sex, drugs, and alcohol and was quite the cocky athlete. He felt like he was invincible. Whatever John wanted, John got, all because of his pitching ability.

During John's senior year, it wasn't only colleges trying to recruit him, but major league baseball teams as well. He was on television, signing autographs, talking to major leagues, and pitching over ninety-five miles per hour. It seemed like life couldn't get any better.

Sometimes, for no reason, John would have bouts of depression; feelings of abandonment, shame, and guilt would haunt him in his dreams or thoughts. When that happened, he would get up, go get a beer and drink until he would pass out. During his senior year those thoughts started haunting him more often.

The day finally came when John had made the decision to forego college and sign with the pros. His dad and sister were so proud of him as he signed his first major league contract in front of all of the local news cameras and local and state newspapers.

Being in the big leagues meant lots of spending money that John had no idea how to handle. It meant lots of pretty women who would leave their names and phone numbers in his message box at the hotel before the team would even get into their town, and it meant the availability of drugs and alcohol at any time, day or night.

John had some elbow problems along the way, but after each of his two surgeries, he came back even stronger than before. He was in total control, except over some of his emotions. Johnny had a terrible temper that got him into lots of fights. He loved fighting, and the least little thing would send him into a rage! Johnny won most all of his fights. He was 6'5" and weighed 240 pounds. Not many guys could whip him or even tried. Most would run when they saw him.

During one particular game, after his second elbow surgery, John was pitching one of his best games ever. Then with no warning, as he released the ball, he heard something pop and his arm felt like someone had shot it with a cannon! He fell to the ground in excruciating pain, rolling from side to side, trying not to cry. He screamed from a gut-wrenching pain that he had never felt before.

After the surgery was over, John asked the surgeon about his period of rehabilitation time. The surgeon looked at John directly in his eyes and said, "Son, I couldn't fix it this time. You're done. Your baseball days are over. Your arm will never heal good enough for you to play major league ball." John looked up at the doctor with tears running down his face. It was the first time he had cried since he was seven years old, when his mom left. He mumbled, "Doc, what am I going to do? Baseball is my life. That's who I am. Without baseball, I don't even know who John is!" The doctor wrapped his arms around this big guy, who, at that moment, needed the unconditional love of a father. For those few minutes, John melted into the doctor's chest and felt like a little boy again, just wanting someone to accept him, tell him it was going to be all right and to give him a secure place to call home.

John realized he needed to make some dramatic changes in his life if he was going to find a new identity. He decided to quit the sex, drugs, and alcohol and make all new friends in order to start over. It wasn't easy, but it was necessary for his peace of mind. He called an old friend he had known briefly from another high school, a guy who was different. He was a good baseball player, but was more than that. He was a man of character. He knew who he was and didn't feel it necessary to prove his manhood by having sex or getting drunk or doing drugs. His name was Calvin, and he was a Christian. John didn't have to elaborate on the phone to Calvin about who he was. Everyone, including Calvin, knew who John was. He was famous in his town, especially with athletes. Calvin struck up a relationship with John, inviting him to church, to Bible study, and to join the church softball team. Of course, they won their league that first year John was playing for them and every year after that. He was learning so much more from them about life than they were learning from him on the softball field.

They taught John that he had a heavenly Father who loved him unconditionally, a Father Who was for him and not against him, and Who didn't care if he was a baseball star or not. He learned that when he followed God's Word, he was blessed, like the day he got a job working with youth at a local church. Life was sweet as a Christian and John was thriving. He was even working on his temper problems.

One of the rare nights when John was alone and feeling depressed, he decided to call an old high school girlfriend to see if she wanted to come over and hang out with him. She already had plans, but said she would call her sister, who was known for living on the wild side. Her sister jumped at the chance to be with John. That evening as they talked and got to know one another a little better, they became aware of a physical attraction to one another. John only meant to kiss her and hold her, but one thing led to another and they ended up having sex. When they finished, a strange sensation came over John. Something told him that he had just fathered a child. Ignoring that voice, John walked her to the door, kissed her goodbye, and intended to never see or call her again.

Six months later John got a call from this same girl, the only one he had had sex with in two years. She told him she was pregnant and the child was his. Deep down inside he knew that what she told him was true, because he remembered the voice that spoke to him the night this baby was conceived. Just to be sure, though, he insisted on a paternity test when the child was born. As he already suspected, the test turned out positive. John was the father of a baby boy.

He was a very proud dad, but he was also very depressed. He had promised himself that he would never bring a child into this world without a mother and a father who loved each other and would stay married and never put their kid though a divorce as he had suffered. He and the mother of his child didn't love each other and they hardly knew each other. They were only a "hook up," a one-night stand, nothing more and nothing less.

John wanted to be a good dad. He had custody of his baby boy on the weekends and worked construction during the week. One particular night he could not get his three–month old son to stop crying, no matter what he did. John was exhausted from work and frazzled, and his inability to quiet his son made a feeling of dark depression begin to creep over him.

John had been in plenty of fights in the past, but he had no idea that he was getting ready to be in a battle like he had never experienced before. This particular night John would be in the most serious fight of his life. It wouldn't be a physical fight like all the others. This one would be a spiritual battle. The stakes were the very highest: his very own life would be the prize!

As John unsuccessfully tried and tried to quiet his child, those demons of abandonment, shame, and guilt took advantage of his state of mind. They mustered their troops to visit him once again. This time their voices were especially strong in John's mind. They sarcastically mocked him by saying, "How do you think you are ever going to be a decent father? You can't even get him to stop crying! You're a loser, John; you're a nothing! You'll never be able to provide a stable home for your son. You're not even married, and what's more, who would want to marry you anyway! You're going to give this son a worse life than you had! Your son, and everyone else, would be better off if you were dead!"

John was sweating all over as his hands reached for the pistol he kept in his nightstand. He leaned over his son on the bed and with tears dropping on the crying baby's face, he said, "I love you, son, but I don't know how to be a dad. You'll be better off this way. Someone will take care of you who knows a lot more than me or your mother."

As John put the gun to his head, the Holy Spirit spoke to his soul and said, "Why don't you call your friend, Calvin? He's always been there for you. He can help you." The demons continued to try and seal the deal, whispering, "What's the matter, John, can't you even succeed at killing yourself? You are such a baby!" The Holy Spirit spoke to his soul again but this time with Scripture: "Johnny, I love you with an everlasting love. You are my son and your son is mine also. Together, we can get through anything. Lean on me and the people I have put in your life to help you. Pick up that phone now and call Calvin!" Demons don't give up easily; they gave their last and final demand to John: "Pull the trigger, you coward! Pull it, you loser!! Pull it NOW!!!"

John threw the gun across the room, picked up the phone, dialed Calvin's number and cried, "Man, I need help!" Calvin said, "Don't worry, I'll be right over." John cried as hard as his baby was crying until Calvin walked in the front door. As soon as he saw him, John felt the Holy Spirit whisper to his mind, "Tell him everything. I've prepared him to be able to handle everything about your past. Your burdens are too heavy to carry any longer.

My yoke is easy. You and Calvin are going to take your burdens to me in prayer."

For the first time since John was a child, he shared with Calvin his most haunting memories. He held nothing back. Calvin just listened. When John finished, he said, "Can I pray with you? God can carry your burdens. You no longer need to." They bowed their heads in prayer.

That night was the beginning of John's healing both in his spirit and in his soul(which the Bible says is our mind, emotions, and intellect). His demons no longer had power over him because he had told someone his darkest secret. They could not torment him through his silence any longer.

When John's son was less than two years old, John came to interview for a job with Project SOS. Calvin had been working with us for several years and talked his friend into applying for a full time mentoring position. Our team of interviewers couldn't help but see the beautiful heart John possessed and the tremendous empathy and concern he had for children. We knew immediately that he could use his athletics to first get the students' attention, and then use his gift of mercy to listen to their problems and help encourage them. He was hired on the spot as a full time mentor. It didn't pay much compared to the booming construction business in Florida, but John wanted and needed a purpose for his life and in his profession.

Our first week of training consists of designing our personal testimonies. I always share with our team that in order to change people's destructive behaviors, they must first reach their hearts. After reaching their hearts, they will be able to change their attitudes. Once their attitudes have been changed, positive behavioral change will soon follow. Then they are able to lead teenagers into making healthy choices for their lives. There can be no getting it out of order if they truly want to change their youth culture for the better. I say to them, "The most powerful weapon a person possesses is his or her own personal testimony."

So, the next several days were spent designing their personal testimonies. As each mentor was individually working on the personal testimony that would be shared with thousands of teens, John went to Calvin, the coordinator of the mentors, and said, "I think I'm supposed to share my testimony about being molested as a young boy." Calvin said, "Then go for it. You can do it, John; remember, you're not alone. He'll help you every step of the way."

John spent several days designing his own personal testimony. On the final day, each mentor and presenter stood in front of our entire staff and shared their personal lives with us. We always require each person to come up with a visual that will help students remember their testimony. When it came time for John to present his story, he held up an old baseball with the strings hanging down and started talking openly about all he had gone through. When he got to the part that he had never shared before with anyone other than Calvin, he broke down and started to sob. The entire staff gathered around him, hugged him, prayed for him, and reassured him that he could do it. After a little while, he was able to finish all of his testimony. As he talked about the new person he had become without the sex, drugs, and alcohol, he pulled a brand new baseball out of the old one and said, "I look like this now. I'm brand new, and you can have a brand new start today too, if you want to."

John has mentored thousands of teenagers. He has shared his testimony freely in many schools. In addition, he has had his soul restored by the Holy Spirit and the

Christians God brought into his life. With God's help, he won the hardest battle he ever had to face: the battle to surrender all of himself, including his memories. As he allowed God to recycle the garbage in his life, he was then ready to help others begin to heal their own lives. I thank God for John. He is truly more than a conqueror. He is no longer a victim; he is a victor in every area.

John received full custody of his son before he was two years old. He is an awesome father and his son is a very happy, well-adjusted, little boy. John and his mother (who had once deserted her family) have restored their relationship. She is a great help to John with his son.

**One out of six boys and one out of three girls will be molested by the time they reach age eighteen. It is NEVER the victim's fault, and they need to tell a trusted adult who will do something about it immediately.**


## Lessons learned:

1. We are truly in a spiritual battle for the body, soul, and spirit of every human being, especially our young people.
2. Children cannot take care of themselves. They need supervision, nurturing, and safety.
3. Not all adults can be trusted, especially now with the privacy of the Internet as a source of temptation to many. Pedophiles are very manipulative, worming their way into the hearts of children prior to molesting them.
4. Our value is not in "who" we are, what we look like, what we can do, or what we own. Our value is in "whose" we are. When we ask Jesus Christ into our hearts, we become children of God, the Creator of the universe. We then have the right to be called sons and

daughters of the King, and we need to see ourselves as He sees us: in an entirely new light. Know that "we can do all things through Christ that strengthens us."

5. God gives all of us gifts and talents. Practicing those gives us identity and self-worth among our peers and sphere of influence.
6. God sends people into our lives to help us. Allow them to help. They will be blessed when you do.
7. Eventually, God restores all relationships, even the most broken and hurtful ones.
8. Addictions are a coverup for feelings of low self-worth and past pain. The cure is to know Jesus Christ personally, live a surrendered life for Him, and know who you are in Him through knowing what His Word, the Bible, says about you.

## Scriptures to learn:

- And we know that all things work together for good to those that love God, and to those who are the called according to His purpose (Romans 8:29).
- (Jesus is talking about people who hurt children): But whoever causes one of these little ones who believe in Me to stumble, it would be better for him if a millstone were hung around his neck, and he were thrown into the sea (Mark 9:42).
- Be angry and do not sin: do not let the sun go down on your wrath, nor give place to the devil (Ephesians 4:26-27).
- Let all bitterness, wrath, anger, clamor, and evil speaking be put away from you, with all malice. And be kind to one another, tenderhearted, forgiving one another, even as God in Christ forgave you (Ephesians 4:31-32).

- For nothing is secret that will not be revealed, nor anything hidden that will not be known and come to light (Luke 8:17).
- For we must all appear before the judgment seat of Christ, that each one may receive the things done in the body, according to what he has done, whether good or bad (2 Corinthians 5:10).
- If anyone is in Christ, he is a new creation; old things have passed away; behold, all things have become new (2 Corinthians 5:17).
- "For the weapons of our warfare are not carnal but mighty in God for pulling down strongholds, casting down arguments and every high thing that exalts itself against the knowledge of God, bringing every thought into captivity to the obedience of Christ, and being ready to punish all disobedience when your obedience is fulfilled (2 Corinthians 10:4-6).
- Therefore, I take pleasure in infirmities, in reproaches, in needs, in persecutions, in distresses, for Christ's sake. For when I am weak, then I am strong (2 Corinthians 12:10).

# INSIDE OUT...

Inside out and
Outside in
That is the way
That God begins
To heal us...
He chooses first to start
Dealing with the issues
Of our divided hearts.
Inside out and outside in
Very topsy-turvy
The ways of God are marvelous
And often very nervy.
No one but God can touch
Our hearts in such a special way,
And woo us with His endless love
Which leads us to obey.
He wounds us to heal us;
Now to the ear that makes no sense.
God is not bound by time...
He speaks in perfect tense.
From the beginning to eternity
God is always working toward
Restoring His creation
To Himself... the risen Lord...
So even in the pain of
Our disobedience and sin,
The Father God is drawing us
To repentance so that then
He can restore us
Once again...
to He who loves us beyond measure...
The framer of eternity...

Katherine Denham Osgood

# FINDING MR. RIGHT

Sue grew up in a beautiful neighborhood with two parents who loved each other and their children. Sue's father was an airline pilot, so she rarely had much time to spend with him. When he saw her, he would always tell her how beautiful her curly blonde hair and blue eyes were. She missed her daddy very much when he was away.

When Sue was in middle school, she set a goal to be well-liked and popular. The popular girls were not doing the kinds of things her parents would have approved of, so she started telling little white lies about whom she was hanging out with and where she was going.

In high school Sue became a cheerleader, got a boyfriend, and started going to parties and spending the night on weekends at some friend's house. Sue's parents knew nothing of her new social life. Not even Sue knew how much it would affect her life when she started dabbling in smoking cigarettes, drinking, and sleeping with her boyfriend. All Sue really wanted was to be popular and have a guy tell her that she was pretty and that he loved her.

Every weekend after the football game there was a big party, and Sue was not one to miss a party! She was a great dancer, lots of fun, and was the life of the party, especially when she had been drinking or doing drugs. Somehow Sue was able to keep her grades up and was accepted to the University of Florida.

Her freshman year was merely an extension of her social life in high school except there were new faces and lots more guys to meet. It was much easier to attend parties in college, because she didn't have to lie to her parents about where she was going or whom she was with on the weekends. In fact, at college there was a party somewhere in the town every night of the week.

Sue decided to major in biology so she could go into pre-med after graduation. She loved health class and was a fanatic when it came to her health, including diet, appearance, and protection. She always used condoms whenever she had sex. She was also on the pill, so she wouldn't mess up her life by getting pregnant. She figured that when it came to sex, she was in total control and had nothing to worry about. She never knew when she would hook-up with a cute guy after a fraternity party or after one of the football games, so she never went anywhere without protection. Sex, to her, had become a recreational sport and no one was getting hurt, because she was smart enough to use protection.

One day during Sue's freshman year, while she was taking a shower, she felt some small, hard bumps in her genital area. She ignored them and went on with her studying, partying and having fun. A month later, she became quite sick and felt blisters in her genital area. That scared her enough to go to the university clinic.

She walked to the clinic, which was about a mile from her dorm, and then waited for over an hour until a very serious nurse took her to an examining room. Sue was so scared she thought about leaving and never coming back, but realized that her problem would only get worse. It seemed like she had been waiting hours for her test results, but in reality it had only been a few minutes. Sue's hands were sweaty and her face was a flushed, bright red.

After running some tests on Sue, the nurse returned to the room where she was anxiously waiting. In a very stern voice the nurse said, "Young lady, you have contracted three sexually transmitted diseases. First, you have Chlamydia, which I can cure by giving you medication, but you may have had the disease for a long time. It may have scarred your tubes, so you might not be able to bear children." Susan had always wanted to be a mother and raise a family. The thought of that not happening pierced her heart like a surgeon's knife. She started to cry. The nurse looked at her and went on, "You have genital herpes which I can give you medicine for, but you'll have outbreaks of it for the rest of your life. It is a viral infection, so there is no cure for it like there is for Chlamydia. The third STD you have is not curable either, but I can burn the warts off today. You will have to return in two weeks to be rechecked to see if more warts have appeared. These warts are caused from HPV, human papillomavirus, which is a disease that you can catch by skin-to-skin contact. Condoms don't stop that one! You will need to have a pap smear done every six months from now on to make sure you don't get cervical cancer." As the nurse finished giving Sue the horrible news, she concluded, "By the way, nuns don't get these diseases!"

After having the warts burned off, Sue looked for her clothes, trying desperately to see through her tears.. She had cried through the entire procedure. It felt like someone had put a hot curling iron between her legs!

Sue had to walk a mile back to the dorms, humiliated, depressed, and all alone. During the entire walk she was in excruciating pain. She had to stop about every hundred yards, because the rubbing of her clothes to her burned skin was killing her! As her tears continued to fall on her shirt, she vowed to never have sex again as long as she lived. She felt very dirty and nasty and was filled with feelings of regret, embarrassment, and shame.

The next day Sue's sorrow turned to anger. She had used protection every time she had sex. How could this have happened to her? Who was it that gave her these diseases? Did that guy know he was infected? Why didn't someone tell her about HPV and that condoms could not protect her? She wanted answers and wanted them right then!

Sue kept her commitment to abstinence, but her anger kept growing. One day a person in college ministry invited her to a Bible study. She went because she had nothing else to do that evening, since she was avoiding the party scene. She didn't want to end up drunk and having sex like she had done so many other times before. So she accepted the invitation to the Bible study.

That night was the beginning of her first relationship of genuine true love. She found out that God loved her so much that He sent His only Son to die for the sins she had committed. Sue knew all too well about her sins. After all, she had the STDs and emotional scars as reminders. What she didn't know, until she attended the Bible study, was that she was forgiven and loved unconditionally by a Father who would always be there for her and never leave her or forsake her. As Sue's faith grew, her anger started to disappear.

During the last semester of her senior year, she did her internship at a local high school teaching biology. One day during the orientation for interning at the high school, she saw a gorgeous, tall, dark, and handsome young man. He noticed her and started to talk to her at the break. She and Don became very good friends during that semester of internship. He would write Sue the most beautiful poems. She also learned that he was a Christian, just like her. He was a baseball star at the University of Florida and was going to be a coach after graduation. Don was falling in love with his best friend, Sue, and she was feeling the same thing for him.

Sue knew she had to tell Don about her diseases. She was so embarrassed and fearful, but she knew that she owed him the chance to walk out of the relationship before it became more serious. She asked Don to come to her apartment for dinner, because she wanted to talk to him about something very important. He was so excited because he was looking for an opportunity to ask her to marry him. That evening seemed like the perfect time. His coaching and playing schedule frequently kept him on the road, but that particular Saturday night he would be home. He went to the local jewelry store and purchased Sue a beautiful engagement ring. He bought her flowers and candles so the mood would be absolutely perfect.

After they had a delicious dinner, she nervously said to Don, "I need to tell you something that I have never told anyone before. Please don't say a word until after I tell you, then I will understand if you get up and walk out that door."

Don was not ready for what he was about to hear. He had wanted to do the talking and ask Sue to marry him. What on earth would she have to tell him that would make him want to walk out the door, he wondered. His mind raced with the possibilities: ***I'll bet she's divorced and*** *didn't know how to tell me. Maybe she's not going to graduate with her class and is embarrassed to tell me she's failing. Surely she doesn't have another boyfriend! She couldn't do that to me, could she?* His thoughts kept racing faster and faster while he waited for her to speak.

Sue hesitated to say anything, looking down at the table where the dinner plates still sat before being cleared. As she stared at the pattern on the tablecloth, she said a small silent prayer that went something like this: *Please God, help me. Allow the words to come out of my mouth, and if it is your will, help Don have mercy on me. In Jesus name, I pray.* Then she began to tell her "Mr. Right" about her past and her contagious, sexually transmitted diseases. As she spoke, she started to cry. She was so ashamed to have to tell him the horrible news. What would he think of her? When she had finished, she said, "I'll understand if you walk out that door now. You are free to go."

Sue heard Don push back his chair and get up from the table. She couldn't look up and see him leave. That would be way too painful, so she kept starring at the tablecloth, never lifting her head. Those voices of condemnation started to say to her mind, *See what you've done. No one will ever want you now. You could have lied and this wouldn't be happening, you stupid girl.*

She expected to hear the door close any second, but instead, she felt Don's arms wrap around her shoulders. He drew her head into his chest and just held her tightly while she cried. She soon heard his voice speak to say, "Sue, we'll get through this together. I'm so sorry that happened to you. I love you, and nothing is going to change that." Right then, Sue remembered hearing those same words from Jesus Christ, to her heart, one night when she was alone after Bible study. Don truly was MR. RIGHT sent from heaven to be her soul mate. She knew that any man who would stay with her, even though he might never have children, could get herpes from her, and would probably contract HPV, must definitely be sent by God!

After she stopped crying, Don released his hold on her, dropped down to one knee, pulled the ring out of his pocket said, "Sue, I love you, and I want to spend the rest of my life with you. Will you please marry me?"

Sue and Don did get married, and the grace of God has been so evident in their lives. It seems that Don's family has immunity to the measles virus. Herpes is in the measles family, so he is immune to catching it from Sue! Also, after Sue attended a healing service where she was prayed for to be cured from her STDs, she has not had any more outbreaks of herpes or warts, and her pap smear tests have shown no signs of pre-cancerous cells caused by HPV. In addition, having Chlamydia did not cause her to be infertile. They have one son.

After recruiting and coaching at the college level, Don is now a sports agent for professional ball players. Sue spent two years speaking to teenagers with Project SOS, and she and Don plan to return to Jacksonville soon so she can work for us again. Sue and Don have spoken nationally to Christian groups, sharing their testimony.

## Lessons learned:

1. Condoms don't stop all STDs.
2. Saving sex for marriage will allow you to have total freedom from diseases and regrets.

3. God has chosen the person you are going to spend the rest of your life with. Wait for His perfect timing and perfect mate. Being popular can be very costly if it means making unhealthy choices.
4. Your grades are only one indicator of how well you are doing. There are many others, some more important than grades.

## Scriptures to learn:

- Have no fellowship with the unfruitful works of darkness, but rather expose them (Ephesians 5:11).
- Fornication (sex outside of marriage) and all uncleanness or covetousness, let it not even be named among you...neither filthiness, nor foolish talking, nor coarse jesting, which are not fitting, but rather giving of thanks (Ephesians 5:3-4).
- Children, obey your parents in the Lord, for this is right. Honor your father and mother, which is the first commandment with promise: that it may be well with you and you may live long on the earth (Ephesians 6:1-3).
- Love suffers long and is kind; love does not envy; love does not parade itself, is not puffed up; does not behave rudely, does not seek its own, is not provoked, thinks no evil; does not rejoice in iniquity, but rejoices in the truth; bears all things, believes all things, hopes all things, endures all things. Love never fails (1 Corinthians 13:4-8).
- Do not be deceived: evil company corrupts good habits." (1 Corinthians 15:33).
- Lying lips are an abomination to the Lord, but those who deal truthfully are His delight (Proverbs 12:22).
- Do not be deceived, God is not mocked; for whatever a man sows, that he will also reap. For he who sows to

his flesh will of the flesh reap corruption, but he who sows to the spirit will of the Spirit reap everlasting life (Galatians 6:7-8).

- Is anyone among you sick? Let him call for the elders of the church, and let them pray over him, anointing him with oil in the name of the Lord. And the prayer of faith will save the sick, and the Lord will raise him up. And if he has committed sins, he will be forgiven. (James 5:14-15).
- …They (those who believe in Jesus) will lay hands on the sick, and they will recover (Mark 16:18).

# FROM FLAME TO FORTUNE

Raging forest fires destroy acres of land;

That any good could come from it is hard to understand.

Yet it does… fresh growth very soon appears;

Then the re-birth process becomes a bit more clear…

Full-established forests often get bogged down with
many vines and weeds,

choking out needed resources which the large trees need;

The fire strips away all that undergrowth

and then fresh new outcrops everywhere suddenly begin;

so with human lives… sometimes destructive "fires" burn

and what seems like utter devastation

is a fresh new chance to learn the ways of God and turn

from earthly things managed well… those fires can
restore us to the King…

so when the heat is on…things are not all bad;

it may open brand new possibilities
you never would have had…

Katherine Denham Osgood

# A TRUE CONQUEROR IN AN OVERWHELMING SOCIETY

Nancy works with teenagers: listening, encouraging, helping, mentoring and empowering them to become leaders for their youth culture. She has worked with teens who are juvenile offenders; teens attending the best private schools; and of course, average kids just looking for someone to listen to them. She knows it doesn't matter how much money they have, what they have done or not done, or where there have been. She knows that what matters is for them to learn that they are all uniquely created individuals needing to give and receive unconditional love.

Nancy knows words either create life or create death. She never speaks badly about someone else or to someone else. Yes, she has the guts to correct someone if they are making wrong choices, but she knows that mistakes are only temporary and gossip hurts. What she gives is something that teenagers find too little of: a listening ear and words of encouragement.

Nancy graduated from Old Dominion University and went straight into working with troubled teens at a boot camp environment. She is Hispanic and beautiful yet very humble. She loves her family and returned home to live with them after college. When she smiles, she lights an entire room. She doesn't judge others, but instead looks at the hearts of others. She is a strong Christian and has remained a virgin for all of her twenty-five years. You might be asking, ***How does she do it?***

You might be thinking, ***Her life has been easy, that's how she has done it.*** Wrong! Nancy is a conqueror in an overwhelming society. She knows "whose" she is and what God's Word says about who she is. She knows God has a purpose for her life, and that purpose is to help teenagers. God's purpose for her might change as her life changes. Someday Nancy will probably get married and start a family, but for right now, she is doing what God has called her to do.

Nancy comes from a large, Hispanic family. There were always plenty of cousins running around at family get-togethers. She was very trusting and loving and thought all adults loved her and were there to protect her.

When she was seven years old, a grown man, who was a friend of her father's, molested her. Afterwards she felt dirty, hurt, and confused. Because children cannot reason like adults and blame themselves for everything that happens to them, Nancy blamed herself. Like most children who have been molested, she thought she had done something wrong to cause this man to do what he had done. She didn't know until much later that her older female cousins were also being molested by the same man on a regular basis. The trusting little girl that Nancy had been became a suspicious child who thought that any male figure was going to hurt her. She thought that the way one man had treated her was the way all men would treat her.

Nancy saw her cousins grow up too quickly, and she didn't want to follow in their footsteps. They were sleeping around with guys, looking for love in all the wrong places, and acting out from being molested. She saw one of her cousins get pregnant at an early age and is now the single mother of three children. Each one of her children has a different father.

Nancy decided to take another route. She knew she wanted better for her life than what she saw her cousins settling for. She started to establish and focus on goals: to do well in high school so she could go to a good college, to stop dating just anyone who would ask her out, and to be very selective in choosing friends. She also set physical boundaries in her dating relationships. Before setting those boundaries, she had always found herself going too fast, too quickly with guys she barely knew. She knew that she deserved respect and wouldn't settle for less. She joined a good church youth group and found friends with similar goals and standards. Having friends with values of her own was key to her success. She also found mentors who would help her stay on track, give her good advice, and listen to her when she needed them. She stayed focused on these goals and talked to her mentors, especially during hard times.

Nancy decided that she would believe God's Word about who He said she was, and to not be concerned with what other people thought or said or what Hollywood wanted her to become. She discovered, through the Bible, that she was a daughter of the King of the universe. She was royalty and started to program her thinking to see herself as that. When you are royalty, you are not better than anyone else, but you do have rights and privileges that others don't get to enjoy.

## Our Rights as Sons and Daughters of the King:

- Favor from God and other people
- Victory through life's battles instead of defeat
- Protective angels; no longer any need to fear
- Eternal life: not having to worry about where I'm going when I die
- Forgiveness from all past, present and future sins; no longer shame, guilt or fear about my past
- Courage to do whatever He asks of me, and knowing He will do it through me, using me as His empty vessel
- Wisdom and discernment; not falling into traps set for me by the evil one, but instead exposing them
- Strength in place of weakness
- Purpose and a plan for my life; not just existing day by day wondering what life is all about
- Answered prayer instead of wishful thinking
- Love for God and others because He first loved me
- Faith that all things will work out for my good, because God is in control, not me
- Hope for my future; not fear of tomorrow
- Peace in my innermost parts instead of anxiety
- Kindness toward others instead of hate, jealousy, or envy
- Joy in my heart in place of anger and negative thinking
- Patience with myself and others, knowing God is not finished with any of us yet
- Self-control instead of being controlled by others or my circumstances
- Perseverance: the ability to stick with something and not quit

## Lessons learned:

1. Setting and focusing on goals is the key to success.
2. Knowing, believing, and memorizing what God's Word says about you will program your mind for success.
3. Smiling warms people's hearts. Do more of it.
4. Pray about everything and trust God instead of worrying about your circumstances.
5. Speak words of encouragement instead of gossip and negativity.
6. Family is important and needs to be appreciated.
7. You can overcome anything with God's help and healing.
8. You are who God says, not what the culture wants you to be.
9. Memorize some Bible verses that will encourage you.

## Scriptures to learn:

- The works of the flesh are evident, which are: adultery, fornication, uncleanness, lewdness, idolatry, sorcery, hatred, contentions, jealousies, outbursts of wrath, selfish ambitions, dissensions, heresies, envy, murder, drunkenness, revelries, and the like ... those that practice such things will not inherit the kingdom of God (Galatians 5:19-21).
- The fruit of the Spirit is love, joy, peace, longsuffering, kindness, goodness, faithfulness, gentleness, self-control (Galatians 5:22-23).
- If a man (person) is overtaken in any trespass (sin), you who are spiritual restore such a one in a spirit of gentleness, considering yourself lest you also be tempted (Galatians 6:1).

- Do not be deceived, God is not mocked; for whatever a man sows, that he will also reap. For he who sows to his flesh will of the flesh reap corruption, but he who sows to the spirit will of the Spirit reap everlasting life (Galatians 6:7-8).
- Let us not grow weary while doing good, for in due season we shall reap if we do not lose heart. Therefore, as we have opportunity, let us do good to all, especially to those who are of the household of faith (Galatians 6:9-10).
- God resists the proud, but gives grace to the humble (James 4:6).
- Humble yourselves in the sight of the Lord, and He will lift you up (James 4:10)
- Do not speak evil of one another, brethren. He who speaks evil of a brother (a fellow Christian) and judges his brother, speaks evil of the law and judges the law…There is one Lawgiver, who is able to save and to destroy. Who are you to judge another (James 4:11-12)?
- Do not grumble against one another, brethren, lest you be condemned. Behold, the Judge is standing at the door (James 5:9)!
- Death and life are in the power of the tongue, and those who love it will eat its fruit (Proverbs 18:21).

# UNIQUE DESIGN

God called, and God assigned.
Spirit led and God designed.
There is no script for His special plan.
But as you're guided by His hand,
you see His fingerprint all through.
Oh… that He ended up with you
is no mistake… no act of chance!…
As you trust in Him, He will enhance
all you are into so much more…
But know that you are in a war…
and all those voices, loud and strong
directing you to just fit in… belong.
That is compromise…your enemy.
The Father says: "Come, follow me."
His ways are higher by far than mine…
and I submit fully to His design…

Katherine Denham Osgood

# THE HIGH COST OF REBELLION

S he was the third daughter of a pastor and his wife. Her two older sisters did everything right, at least in Shannon's mind. When she arrived at middle school the teachers immediately started to compare her with her older sisters who were excellent students. Shannon wanted her own identity. She also liked being different, walking on the edge, so to speak, and being noticed, regardless of the reasons why.

She started to sneak out at night when she was thirteen to go to parties where there were older kids. One night she met Cliff. He was older, "drop-dead" gorgeous, and all the girls liked him, but that night, Cliff only had eyes for Shannon. They went upstairs to an empty bedroom. Of course, the parents weren't at home and had no idea about the party at their house. They started making out, and one thing led to another. Shannon stopped before actually having sex. She wasn't going to go ALL the way until her wedding night. Cliff rolled her over, looked right into her eyes, and said in an angry voice, "If you ever do that to me again, I'll rape you." Shannon knew he meant it, but she still liked him. It must have been the challenge she saw in Cliff, or maybe it was the way other girls were jealous of her because Cliff was a hunk, or maybe it was the attention she was getting because she had no fear and other middle school kids did.

Shortly after that night, Shannon agreed to sneak out of her house and meet Cliff. He wanted to make out again and so did she. This time, when things got carried away, she knew that he would rape her, so instead of being violently raped, she just laid there and let him have sex with her. When he had finished, he stood up and said, "Yes, I got the pastor's daughter!" Shannon held back her tears until she had slipped back in the window of her bedroom. After all, she certainly wasn't going to give Cliff the satisfaction of knowing that she was upset and that he had won!

As Shannon cried herself to sleep that night, she thought about how horrible it was losing her virginity to such a creep. She had wanted to save herself but didn't know how. No one had taken the time to share with her about refusal skills or boundaries so she could have avoided getting into that situation in the first place. Her heart was filling with regret, shame, and disappointment, especially in herself. She knew that she had been had, used, and discarded, and she hated Cliff for what he had done to her. He was nothing more than a total, worthless, dirtbag in her mind.

Shannon didn't dare tell her parents about what had happened. She just started to become more rebellious. She kept sneaking out, going to parties, getting wasted, and then sneaking back into her bedroom. Finally her parents found out. They knew something had changed in their daughter. They could no longer talk with her. She would blow up any time they questioned what she was doing or where she was going.

Soon, Shannon quit trying to hide her rebellion from her parents. She would come home drunk, swear at them, and sleep in the next day. They didn't know what to do, but knew they had to do something and do it very quickly. They were losing their little girl, and Shannon's sisters were not able to help her either. In fact, she was embarrassing and disappointing to her entire family, not to mention her church where her father was the pastor.

Shannon's parents finally gave up and found a boot camp. Upon her arrival, she tried every trick she could think of to get kicked out, but nothing worked. She swore at authority figures, spit on people, tried to sleep around and managed to get a reputation of being BAD. That reputation got her lots of attention but also lots of problems at the same time. The boot camp punished her for her rebellion and made her do hard labor. After several weeks of digging ditches, she decided to obey, not because she wanted to of course, but because the alternative was too hard.

Upon Shannon's graduation from the boot camp, her parents enrolled her in a Christian high school so she could be around Christian kids and have a fresh start. Her father helped her get accepted into the school. Being a pastor does have some benefits. During her first semester, Shannon fell in love with a most gorgeous guy. He loved her too. They were an "item" around campus. Shannon's identity was now changing from "wild" child to "reformed" child. Her boyfriend was a star athlete and everyone thought they were so perfect for each other. They dated for quite some time before becoming sexually active. They had sex for the same reason many teens do: because they wanted to "give each other everything," and they even talked about getting married some day.

Several months later, right before graduation, Shannon learned she was pregnant. She told her boyfriend, and he was shocked. He said, "Shannon, I love you and I'll always be there for you, but I'm not ready to be a father. I want to play ball in college next year." Shannon knew how he felt. After all, she didn't really want to be a mother at seventeen years of age. She suggested they could put the baby up for adoption, but he said, "Then everyone will know, and it might mess up my chances to get a scholarship. Plus, you'll get fat, have morning sickness and have to go through the pain of delivery, not to mention the pain of giving up the baby to someone you don't even know! How about we do the easiest, most economical thing and get an abortion?"

Shannon knew from her upbringing in the church that abortion was taking the life of another person, but she could see no other options. Plus, she didn't want to lose her boyfriend, and she was afraid if she didn't abort the baby, he would leave her.

They somehow raised the necessary $450 dollars from friends who understood their situation and wanted to help. She scheduled the appointment, and she and her boyfriend went together to have the procedure done. It took longer than she thought, and after the procedure was done, she walked back to the waiting room hoping to have her boyfriend hold her while she cried. This was a very big decision they had made together, and she needed him to reassure her that they had made the right choice. When she returned to the waiting room, she couldn't find her boyfriend. She called him on his cell phone; he apologized and told her that he had to leave to go to ball practice. He said, "If I miss practice, my coach will kill me, and I'll lose the scholarship I'm counting on to go to college. You understand, don't you?" Shannon tried to mask her true feelings and put on her game face and voice. "Sure, I understand." Shannon understood a little too well. Her boyfriend put his athletics before her when she needed him most! This was the most horrible day in her life! She realized right then that he really didn't love her as much as she thought he did. From that moment on, Shannon vowed that no one would hurt her again. She left, crying, not only on the visible outside, but also on the invisible inside. She tried to act tough in order to protect her heart from anymore pain. She hurt so badly that she wished she were dead.

Shannon started having nightmares about all of the poor choices she had made in her life, so she tried to cover those feeling with getting high and becoming numb to her true needs. She spent every day drinking, taking drugs, or sleeping around. She was invincible, and no one could touch her. She had shut down emotionally. The only feelings she had left were depression and self-hatred.

After graduation she took a job as a waitress at a local restaurant and bar. She did her job, went out partying after work, and then went home to her apartment, many nights with some guy she didn't even care about. She wasn't concerned about anyone or anything. She was miserable and her life had become one nightmare after another.

One night when she couldn't sleep, Shannon decided that she was ready to end it all. She felt she just couldn't live any longer. She hated God, hated her family, and most of all, she hated herself. She thought, "I'll go to the highest bridge near my apartment and drive off the side before I get to the guard rails. That way no one will know if it was an accident or a suicide." She had her plan all figured out, and she was starting to feel better. She got into her car and drove to the highest bridge nearby. As she approached the bridge, she could see the place where she was to veer off. She wanted to make sure she had enough speed to throw the car from the embankment, so she stepped on the gas, pushing the accelerator all the way to the floor. Right before she turned the wheel to throw her car off the side of the bridge, her cell phone rang. She slowed down to answer it and steered over the bridge instead of down the embankment. She figured that she could drive over the bridge and start again on the other side after she found out who in the world was calling her at 2:00 a.m.! When she answered the call, she heard the voice of an old friend say, "Shannon, something woke me up and said to call you to see if I could help you. Are you okay?" Shannon knew at that moment that someone did care about her. Someone had gotten out of bed at 2:00 a.m. to call her. She knew, in her heart, that God had awakened her old friend because He wanted to use her to save Shannon's life. At that moment, she decided against taking her life and went to her friend's house instead. They spent hours talking. She poured her heart out to this friend that God had called to be there for her. Her friend was a Christian, and she shared some scriptures with Shannon that night:

I have loved you with an everlasting love.
For I am with you to save you and deliver you
(Jeremiah 15:20b).
Heal me, O Lord, and I shall be healed; Save me, and I shall be saved (Jeremiah. 17:14).

Shannon decided that if she wanted different results in her life, then she would need to do something different. So she did. She set out a plan in the form of written goals to get off drugs and alcohol, to become abstinent, to go get tested for STDs and to relocate. She had a sister who lived in Jacksonville, Florida, who encouraged Shannon to move in with her and her family until she got on her feet. She also told Shannon about Project SOS and how it was working with thousands of teens to help them. She told her she would call to see if they would hire her to be a school presenter.

Unfortunately, Shannon's test results for STDs did show up positive for HPV, which is the leading cause of cervical cancer. The doctor treated the pre-cancerous cells and told her to be re-checked every six months.

Shannon started working for Project SOS part-time and a website design company full-time. She also enrolled in a Bible study at a local crisis pregnancy center for girls who have had abortions. There, she met a wonderful support group of girls, many who had made the same decision that she made to change their lifestyles from negative choices to healthy, positive ones. It was there that Shannon learned about the unconditional love and forgiveness God extended to her. She was healed through that study.

Shannon took what had happened to her and used it to effectively change other teens' lives. She was even featured on a local television station during a one-hour program called "Straight Talk." She shared her testimony and told others how they could learn from her mistakes and not go down a similar path. She let the viewers know their lives did matter and that they needed to set boundaries, especially physical ones, to get an accountability partner and to practice the word "no" and mean it. Shannon learned, first hand, the cost of rebellion and dedicated her life to helping thousands of teens learn from her unhealthy choices.

**Lessons to learn:**

1. Tell your parents when traumatic things happen to you so they can get you the help you need. Parents are protectors and will be there for you when you have been traumatized.
2. Anyone can make changes in their lives with a set of written, realistic goals and the desire to achieve them.
3. Understand your value and worth, and don't go down the destructive road that Shannon chose.
4. Believe in yourself that you can do great things, and don't listen to negative talk from yourself or others.
5. Choose your thoughts wisely. You become who you think you are.
6. Speak life-changing words to yourself and to anyone you know who needs to hear a word of encouragement.
7. Know that the purpose of trials is not to break you but to make you. Trials are challenges waiting to be conquered by you. Don't quit. Prove to yourself that you CAN overcome a trial with victory.
8. Be a person of excellence and integrity, and reach out to those who are following your footsteps. Someone is watching and admiring you. Look around to see how you can mentor that person.
9. Don't focus on yourself. That causes discontentment. Focus on others. Be a giver. When you meet other people's need, God will provide for your needs, plus it will make you feel better about yourself.
10. Stay away from people, places or things that make you have a negative attitude. Negativity is very contagious.
11. Happiness, like forgiveness, is a choice.

## Scriptures to learn:

- There is a friend (Jesus) who sticks closer than a brother (Proverbs 18:24).
- Poverty and shame will come to him who distains correction, but he who regards a rebuke will be honored (Proverbs 13:18).
- He who distains instruction despises his own soul, but he who heeds rebukes gets understanding (Proverbs 15:32).
- A friend loves at all times, and a brother is born for adversity (Proverbs 17:17).
- Listen to counsel and receive instruction, that you may be wise in your latter days (Proverbs 19:20).
- Wine is a mocker, strong drink is a brawler, and whoever is led astray by it is not wise (Proverbs 20:1).
- Death and life are in the power of the tongue, and those who love it will eat its fruit (Proverbs 18:21).
- Do not be deceived, God is not mocked; for whatever a man sows, that he will also reap. For he who sows to his flesh will of the flesh reap corruption, but he who sows to the spirit will of the Spirit reap everlasting life (Galatians 6:7-8).

# REFLECTIONS

A perfect huge and wintry moon just lights up the
night.
I marvel at the grace of God to bless us with such a sight…
All creation points to Him, and is a testimony
of
The lengths He will go to draw us in, as partakers of His love.
The moon is not so impressive… it's a great big ball of stone,
A beacon in the night to testify that we are not
alone.
And God understands the frailty of man…
We have no power on our
own….
That is Jesus' plan….
That just like the powerless moon that turns the night aglow…
We'll rest in His able hands confident that our God knows….
Everything about us…there's no hiding things from
Him…
As we die to self, we can then reflect
His light of love that never
dims…

Katherine Denham Osgood

# GOD REWARDS COURAGE

Take a look at Daniel in the Bible. He was only 14 years old when he showed more courage than most adults. He somehow knew that God focuses on what a man is. On the contrary, man focuses on what a man does. God knows that if a person is what he ought to be, he will do what he ought to do.

Daniel's nation was taken into captivity, and Daniel was considered a slave. Even as a slave, Daniel had influence as a leader. He and his three Hebrew friends decided to stand tall by going against King Nebuchadnezzar, who ruled the country. Daniel's rebellion was stated like this: "Where God draws His line, I will draw mine." When God said don't do something, they had the courage to say, "We are not going to do that."

Daniel courageously, yet politely, told the king that He was not allowed to worship the golden idol as the king commanded everyone to do. For that act of rebellion, Daniel was thrown into a den of hungry lions, but God protected him by sending an angel to shut the mouths of all of the lions and put them to sleep. When the king came and looked down into the den of lions, he saw that Daniel was untouched and the lions were asleep. He commanded the guards to bring Daniel out of the den, then had the guards thrown in. The lions leaped up and tore the guards to shreds.

Another example was when the king had Daniel's three friends, Shadrach, Meshach, and Abednego, thrown into a furnace of fire. The furnace was so hot, in fact, that the guards who opened it, to throw the boys in, were burned to death by the heat. Supernaturally, the boys were able to not only survive the hot fire, but they didn't even smell of smoke. In addition, when the furnace door was opened, there was a fourth man in the fire! Jesus was with the three boys protecting them from the flames! Now that's power!

Let's look at the rewards God gave to Daniel and his friends because of the courage they showed in standing for God's Word:

1. Special Physical Strength: After 10 days of eating only vegetables and water instead of the food the king had sacrificed to idols, they looked stronger and better than the rest of the people who ate the rich food. They were given power and strength for doing what was right.

2. Special Intelligence: God gave Daniel, who was only a teenager, knowledge, skill, and wisdom ten times greater than all of the magicians and astrologers throughout the land.

3. Special Insight: Daniel was given the gift of interpreting dreams and visions that we to this day use for end time prophesy to tell us what will happen in God's plan for our lives.

4. Special Influence: Daniel stood before kings and was given honor and trust to be in command because people knew they could count on him to be consistent and not waiver.

5. Special Impact on Others: After seeing Daniel stand up to the king and not compromise, his friends were much more courageous and did the same thing. He became greatly loved by his people, the Hebrews, and became their champion and role model.

**Under pressure at age 14, Daniel took a stand when he was tempted to compromise and said "NO." The rest is history!**

# NOW WHAT???

After reading this book, take time away, just a time for you, God, and nature. Talk to God just like you would talk to your closest friend. He wants to hear from you, and He is NEVER too busy for you. Ask Him to show you the gifts and talents that He has placed inside of you. Ask Him to stir them up and make them large, and then ask Him to show you what He wants you to do with those gifts and talents. You don't have to wait to be used for God's purposes. Ask Him who He wants you to help today. He may just want you to be an encourager to someone at your school who is having a hard time, or He may ask you to start a sexual abstinence revolution among the kids in your class, or on your team, or in your activities.

One thing I know for sure: God doesn't want you to just do nothing. He wants you to walk tall, speak boldly, encourage often, and help someone who is making unhealthy choices. He wants you to have the courage to tell others about the good decisions you have made, and how those decisions have brought you total freedom. If you have been making poor choices, learn from the twelve stories you've just read. Every one of the teens described in this book ended up with painful consequences when they made unhealthy choices. You don't have to repeat mistakes; learn from them. They can be your best teacher in life. Help others to not destroy themselves with the same bad choices. When you work for God, you get unbelievable blessings. He truly takes care of all your needs.

Be proud to let people know that you care about your body, mind, and future. When someone starts bragging about what they did with another person, or what they drank, or what they took that was illegal, jump in with a greater brag about what you are doing to have fun without regret. There are no consequences to doing the right thing. You never have to worry about getting pregnant or getting someone else pregnant, or catching an STD, or having your heart torn out of your chest by someone who says he or she loves you but then leaves you. When you do the right thing, you gain confidence, and you will eventually become a leader whom others look up to and wish they were able to be like. There is enough drama in your life without throwing sex, drugs, alcohol, suicide, violence, or eating disorders into the mix. Be happy, be confident, and be free. You'll have NO regrets that you did.

If you have messed up and have regrets, don't run from God; instead run to Him. He is there to forgive you and to change you. What would happen if a baby messed in its diaper and then ran from the one who could change him? What would that baby smell like after a couple of days? Our lives are no different. When we mess up and run from God, our lives start to stink just like a baby's dirty diaper. Don't be a baby; run to the One who can change you for the better.

Learn the scripture verses that can set you free and help you do the right thing; you will then feel good about yourself and will become the leader God has called you to be. God has written over 700 promises for His children in the Bible. Buy a copy of the book called "Bible Promises for You."

You are His child if you have asked Jesus Christ into your life and have surrendered your life to His purposes. If you have not done that, do it now. Just like talking to a friend, invite Christ into your life and ask Him to be your leader and guide and to forgive you for your past mistakes.

Failure is not an option for someone who is totally surrendered to God. He will make you prosper. If you have surrendered and feel like you are still a failure, you are probably doing one of the following four:

Procrastinating, having a negative attitude, being self-centered, or making excuses to not stand up and do what is right.

Read the following conclusions to get back on the track to success:

- It takes discipline to read the Bible, to memorize the scriptures that speak clearly to you, and to join a church or group that meets regularly.
- Negative attitudes are everywhere you turn. Negative people are not successful people. They are babies who are too weak or too lazy to know how to take control of their minds and obey the Word. We are to take control, think godly thoughts, and accomplish God's purpose for our lives.
- Self-centered people are all about themselves. They focus on the big "me" and are too preoccupied to see other people who have needs and who need encourage-

ment or help. Self-centeredness can result in depression. To get out of depression, focus on others and their needs.

- Weakness can be overcome with strength by practice. Just like how it takes dedication to make your muscles and body strong by going to the gym regularly, it also takes dedication to become strong spiritually. The first time you say "no" to temptation is the hardest. Every time after that becomes easier and easier.

- Remember, it takes 21 days to break a bad habit. Be strong enough for 21 days and you've won! Doing the right thing in this culture takes guts, fortitude, and strength. Memorize 2 Timothy 1:7: "For God has not given us a spirit of fear, but of POWER and LOVE and of a SOUND MIND."

- Now go and change your youth culture for the better. You and God are a majority!

# BOOK EVALUATION

I appreciate your taking the time to read this book and give me your honest opinion. I need your wisdom and feedback so this book can be used as an instrument to reach the hearts of teens throughout the nation.

After reading the book, please fill out the following evaluation for me and send it back to Project SOS, 6850 Belfort Oaks Place, Jacksonville, FL 32216. Your name is optional so please be honest in your response. Thank you, Pam

YES   NO

_____ _____ Did you enjoy this book and did it keep your attention?

_____ _____ Would you recommend this book to your friends?

_____ _____ Did the stories impact your life? If so, which ones do you think were the most meaningful to you? (Use the back of this sheet)

_____ _____ Has this book inspired you to make any commitments for your life or change decisions that you may have made in the past? If so, what will you commit to or change?

YES   NO

_____ _____   Has this book helped you to make a commitment to abstain from sex until marriage and avoid other unhealthy choices? (If you already have made that commitment, did this book reinforce your commitment?)

_____ _____   Do you believe that you are destined to do great things with God's help?

_____ _____   Has this book helped you to want to answer the call God has for your life?

_____ _____   Would you like to help Project SOS change our youth culture for the better? If so, please contact me at (904) 537-4053. Please use the back of this sheet to let me know any other thoughts you may have. Thanks!

Printed in the United States
43791LVS00007BA/1-180